KETO DIET
COOKBOOK FOR BEGINNERS

101 Simple & Tasty Low-Carb, Low-Sugar Recipes to Launch
Your Health Journey | Comprehensive 30-Day Meal Plan |
Full-Color Photos Included.

OLIVIA ROBSON

Disclaimer

The recipes and information in this cookbook are provided as is and may not be fully accurate or applicable to all individuals. Nutritional information is offered as a guide and should not be considered as medical or nutritional advice. While the recipes within this book are designed to support a ketogenic diet, they may not be suitable for everyone. Always consult with a qualified healthcare professional before starting any new diet or health program.

The author and publisher of this book disclaim any liability in connection with the use of this information. It is your responsibility to assess your own dietary needs and seek the advice of a qualified medical professional. No warranty or guarantee of a cure is expressed or implied with any information in this book, nor does the author and publisher recommend any treatments or diets for medical conditions.

TABLE OF CONTENTS

CHAPTER 6: SNACKS & APPETIZERS - PERFECT PICKS FOR BETWEEN MEALS OR SMALL GATHERINGS

CHAPTER 7: DESSERTS - SWEET TREATS WITHOUT THE SUGAR SPIKE

CHAPTER 8: SAUCES AND DRESSINGS - KETO-FRIENDLY ADDITIONS TO ENHANCE ANY MEAL

CHAPTER 9: SHOPPING LIST AND INDEX

INTRODUCTION

Welcome to the beginning of your health transformation! If you're looking to embrace a keto lifestyle but are unsure where to start, "Keto Diet Cookbook for Beginners" is your perfect companion. This book is designed not only to introduce you to the world of ketogenic eating but also to make it enjoyable and sustainable.

In this comprehensive guide, you will find 101 simple and delicious recipes that adhere to the ketogenic principle of low carbohydrates and low sugars while focusing on high fats and moderate proteins. Each recipe has been carefully crafted to ensure it's not only healthful but also flavorful, making your journey into keto as delightful as it is beneficial.

This book is divided into well-organized sections including breakfasts, lunches, dinners, snacks and appetizers, desserts, and sauces and dressings—each offering a variety of dishes that will cater to all tastes and preferences. From hearty breakfasts to satisfy your morning appetite, to sumptuous dinners that you can share with family and friends, each recipe is designed to keep you on track without sacrificing taste or variety.

Accompanying these recipes is a comprehensive 30-day meal plan that provides a structured yet flexible approach to your first month of keto eating. This plan will help you understand the balance of your meal compositions, how to plan your meals throughout the day, and how to adjust portions to meet your specific needs.

Moreover, "Keto Diet Cookbook for Beginners" is visually stunning, with full-color photos accompanying each recipe. These images not only add a visual feast to your meal preparation but also guide you in making each dish an aesthetic success.

Embarking on a diet transformation can be daunting, but with this cookbook, Olivia Robson aims to simplify the ketogenic diet to make it accessible, enjoyable, and most importantly, effective. Whether you're a complete novice in the kitchen or looking to expand your culinary skills, this book promises to be a valuable resource in your keto lifestyle. Let's embark on this health journey together, one tasty recipe at a time!

Happy cooking, Olivia Robson

CHAPTER 1
WELCOME TO THE KETO LIFESTYLE

What is Keto?

Introduction to the Keto Diet
The Keto (short for ketogenic) Diet has gained widespread popularity in recent years as an effective way of eating to promote weight loss, improve overall health, and support long-term wellness. At its core, the Keto Diet emphasizes high-fat, moderate-protein, and low-carbohydrate intake, fundamentally shifting the way your body processes energy.

When carbohydrates are drastically reduced, your body enters a metabolic state called ketosis. In ketosis, the liver converts fats into molecules called ketones, which the body uses for fuel instead of glucose (sugar). This metabolic shift forms the basis of the diet's health benefits, allowing the body to efficiently burn fat for energy.

Core Components of the Keto Diet
The Keto Diet revolves around three main macronutrients: fats, proteins, and carbohydrates, with a specific focus on increasing fat intake while minimizing carbs. Here's a breakdown of the typical macronutrient ratio for a Keto Diet:

- **Fats:** 70-80% of daily caloric intake
- **Proteins:** 15-20% of daily caloric intake
- **Carbohydrates:** 5-10% of daily caloric intake

To achieve these ratios, the diet encourages consuming foods rich in healthy fats (such as avocados, nuts, and oils), moderate amounts of protein (such as meat, fish, and eggs), and very few carbohydrates (primarily from leafy greens and non-starchy vegetables). Processed sugars, grains, and starchy foods like bread, pasta, and potatoes are restricted.

The Keto Diet offers a powerful way to take control of your health through a high-fat, low-carb approach that enhances fat burning, supports cognitive function, and helps manage blood sugar levels. By making small, simple changes to your daily eating habits, you can easily incorporate Keto into your life.

With the right tools—like meal planning, cooking techniques, and a commitment to staying active—the Keto lifestyle can be incredibly rewarding. So take the plunge, embrace this wholesome way of eating, and enjoy the many benefits that come with living a Keto-centric life!

The Comprehensive Benefits of the Keto Diet: A Path to Health and Vitality

The core principles of the Keto diet-limiting carbs and increasing fats-support various aspects of health:

1. **Enhanced Energy Levels:** With fat as the primary fuel source, many people experience steady, sustained energy throughout the day. Unlike carbs, which cause blood sugar spikes followed by crashes, fat provides long-lasting energy without the highs and lows, leading to improved productivity and focus.
2. **Disease Prevention and Management:** Research suggests that the Keto diet can help prevent and manage chronic conditions. For instance, reducing carbohydrate intake improves insulin sensitivity, making the Keto diet highly effective for people with type 2 diabetes. Studies have also shown potential benefits in reducing risks of heart disease, epilepsy, and even neurodegenerative diseases like Alzheimer's and Parkinson's.
3. **Improved Weight Loss:** One of the main reasons people adopt the Keto diet is for weight loss. By drastically cutting carbs, the body turns to its fat stores for energy, leading to faster fat loss. The high-fat content of the diet also promotes satiety, helping to reduce cravings and overall calorie intake. Multiple studies confirm that the Keto diet can lead to greater fat loss compared to low-fat or calorie-restricted diets.

Evidence-Based Health Benefits of the Keto Diet

1. **Blood Sugar and Insulin Regulation:** The Keto diet has been extensively studied for its positive effects on blood sugar control. A 2017 study published in the journal *Diabetes Therapy* found that individuals following a ketogenic diet experienced significantly lower blood sugar levels and improved insulin sensitivity compared to those following a standard low-fat diet. This makes the Keto diet particularly beneficial for people with type 2 diabetes or insulin resistance.
2. **Heart Health:** Contrary to the myth that a high-fat diet is harmful to the heart, the Keto diet can improve cardiovascular health by increasing levels of "good" HDL cholesterol and reducing triglycerides, both of which are associated with a lower risk of heart disease. A study published in *The British Journal of Nutrition* found that participants on a Keto diet had improved cholesterol markers after 24 weeks compared to those on a low-fat diet.
3. **Brain Health:** The brain thrives on ketones, which provide a more stable and efficient source of energy than glucose. This is why people on the Keto diet often report improved focus, mental clarity, and cognitive function. Research even suggests that the Keto diet could have neuroprotective effects, potentially helping to prevent or manage conditions like Alzheimer's.
4. **Epilepsy and Neurological Conditions:** The ketogenic diet was originally developed to treat epilepsy, and it remains one of the most effective dietary therapies for this condition. Studies show that following a strict Keto diet can reduce the frequency and severity of seizures, particularly in drug-resistant epilepsy patients.

Mental and Emotional Benefits of the Keto Diet

In addition to the physical health benefits, the Keto diet has profound effects on mental and emotional well-being:

1. **Improved Mood:** Many individuals experience more stable moods and reduced anxiety on the Keto diet. This is likely due to the elimination of sugar spikes and crashes, which are known to affect mood and energy levels. Furthermore, the brain's preferred use of ketones for energy can lead to enhanced emotional stability.
2. **Better Sleep Patterns:** People following the Keto diet often report improved sleep quality. By reducing carbs and increasing fats, blood sugar fluctuations that can disturb sleep are minimized, resulting in more restful and rejuvenating nights.
3. **Increased Mental Clarity and Focus:** The steady stream of energy provided by fats and ketones supports brain function. Many people notice that they are more productive and experience fewer distractions or "brain fog" while on the Keto diet.

What to eat and what to avoid.

Foods to Eat on the Keto Diet
The cornerstone of the Keto diet is consuming high-fat, moderate-protein, and low-carbohydrate foods. Here is the key food groups encouraged on the Keto diet, along with the reasons why they are beneficial.

1. **Healthy Fats**
Fats are the primary source of energy on the Keto diet, making them essential for achieving ketosis. These fats are derived from natural, unprocessed sources, ensuring they provide sustained energy and satiety.

Examples: Avocados, Olive oil, Coconut oil, Butter (preferably grass-fed), Ghee, Fatty fish (like salmon, mackerel, sardines), Nuts and seeds (almonds, walnuts, flaxseeds, chia seeds), Full-fat dairy (cheese, cream, sour cream)

Nutritional Benefits: Healthy fats provide long-lasting energy and help the body stay in ketosis by maintaining low insulin levels. They also help increase satiety, preventing overeating, and provide essential fatty acids, such as omega-3s, which are vital for brain and heart health.

Practical Tips: When selecting fats, choose unprocessed and cold-pressed oils like extra virgin olive oil for dressings and coconut oil for cooking. Incorporate fatty fish into your diet at least once or twice a week, and snack on nuts or nut butter to boost your fat intake.

2. **Protein-Rich Foods**
While protein is important, it's consumed in moderation on the Keto diet. Adequate protein intake helps build and repair tissues, maintain muscle mass, and promote satiety.

Examples: Meat (beef, pork, lamb, chicken), Fish and seafood (shrimp, crab, tuna), Eggs, Poultry (turkey, duck), Cheese and full-fat dairy

Nutritional Benefits: Protein helps maintain muscle mass during weight loss, supports metabolism, and provides essential amino acids for overall body function. It is also filling, which can help prevent cravings for carbs.

Practical Tips: Opt for grass-fed meats and wild-caught seafood whenever possible for the highest nutritional value. Eggs are an inexpensive, versatile protein source that can be included in any meal, from breakfast to dinner.

3. Low-Carb Vegetables
Non-starchy vegetables are an essential part of the Keto diet because they provide fiber, vitamins, and minerals without significantly increasing carbohydrate intake.

Examples: Leafy greens (spinach, kale, arugula), Cruciferous vegetables (broccoli, cauliflower, Brussels sprouts), Zucchini, Bell peppers, Mushrooms, Asparagus

Nutritional Benefits: These vegetables are nutrient-dense and low in carbs, making them perfect for maintaining ketosis while ensuring the body receives essential nutrients, fiber for digestion, and antioxidants for overall health.

Practical Tips: Incorporate a variety of vegetables to keep meals interesting. Use cauliflower as a low-carb substitute for mashed potatoes or rice and try making zucchini noodles (zoodles) instead of traditional pasta.

4. Nuts and Seeds
Nuts and seeds are high in healthy fats and fiber, making them a great snack option on the Keto diet. However, some nuts are higher in carbs than others, so it's important to choose wisely.

Examples: Almonds, Walnuts, Macadamia nuts, Chia seeds, Flaxseeds, Pumpkin seeds

Nutritional Benefits: Nuts and seeds offer a source of heart-healthy fats, fiber, and plant-based protein. They also provide a satisfying crunch and can be used to add texture to dishes.

Practical Tips: Be mindful of portion sizes as nuts can be calorie dense. Use nut butters as a topping for Keto-friendly desserts or blend them into smoothies for added fat and flavor.

Foods to Avoid on the Keto Diet
The Keto diet requires avoiding foods high in carbohydrates, especially processed and sugary items that can spike insulin levels and knock the body out of ketosis. Here are the primary food groups to avoid or limit:

1. Sugary Foods and Beverages
Sugar and sugary foods are the biggest enemies of ketosis, as they quickly raise blood sugar levels and prevent fat from being used as fuel.

Examples: Sweets and candy, Baked goods (cakes, cookies, pastries), Sugary cereals, soft drinks, Fruit juices, Ice cream

Why Avoid Them: High-sugar foods lead to insulin spikes, which stop ketosis and encourage fat storage. They also contribute to energy crashes, weight gain, and inflammation in the body.

How to Overcome: Cravings for sweets can be managed by using Keto-friendly sweeteners like stevia, erythritol, or monk fruit. Additionally, try creating your own Keto desserts with almond flour and these sweeteners to stay compliant.

2. Grains and Starches
Grains are high in carbohydrates and are to be avoided or greatly minimized on the Keto diet.

Examples: Bread, Pasta, Rice, Oats, Quinoa, Corn, Potatoes

Why Avoid Them: Grains are packed with carbs, which can rapidly raise blood sugar levels, prevent ketosis, and increase fat storage. Even whole grains, while nutritious, contain too many carbohydrates for a strict Keto regimen.

How to Overcome: Replace grains with low-carb alternatives like cauliflower rice, zucchini noodles, or almond flour-based baked goods. This ensures you can still enjoy the texture and experience of traditional foods without the carbs.

3. High-Carb Fruits
While fruits are packed with vitamins and antioxidants, most are too high in sugar to be Keto-friendly.

Examples: Bananas, Apples, Grapes, Mangoes, Pineapples

Why Avoid Them: Fruits like bananas and apples contain large amounts of sugar (fructose), which can quickly add up in carb count, taking you out of ketosis.

How to Overcome: Stick to low-carb fruits like berries (raspberries, strawberries, blackberries), which are lower in sugar and rich in fiber and antioxidants.

4. Processed and Refined Foods
Processed foods often contain hidden sugars, unhealthy fats, and preservatives that are harmful to health and not conducive to the goals of the Keto diet.

Examples: Chips and crackers, Baked goods, Processed meats (sausages, hot dogs with fillers), Prepackaged meals

Why Avoid Them: Processed foods contain low-quality fats, additives, and often hidden sugars, which hinder ketosis, promote inflammation, and lack nutritional value.

How to Overcome: Prepare your meals at home to have control over ingredients and quality. If you're craving something crunchy, opt for Keto-friendly snacks like pork rinds, cheese crisps, or roasted nuts.

Reading Food Labels: Key Ingredients to Watch Out For
When following the Keto diet, reading food labels becomes crucial to ensure you're avoiding hidden carbs and sugars. Here's what to look for:

1. **Net Carbs:** Focus on the "net carbs" by subtracting fiber from the total carbohydrate count. Keto dieters typically aim for 20-50 grams of net carbs per day.
2. **Added Sugars:** Check for ingredients like corn syrup, dextrose, fructose, and maltodextrin. Even "healthy" sugars like agave syrup, honey, or maple syrup can spike blood sugar.

3. **Artificial Sweeteners:** Be cautious with artificial sweeteners like aspartame or sucralose, as they can affect insulin levels or cause digestive issues. Stick to Keto-approved options like erythritol and stevia.
4. **Ingredients Lists:** Choose foods with short, recognizable ingredient lists. Avoid products with multiple preservatives or fillers.

Practical Tips for Incorporating the Keto Diet

Adopting the Keto Diet can feel daunting at first, but with a few simple changes and strategies, you can seamlessly integrate it into your routine. Here are some practical tips for beginners:

1. **Start with Simple Swaps**
   - **Bread:** Swap traditional bread for lettuce wraps or low-carb alternatives like almond or coconut flour-based bread.
   - **Pasta:** Replace regular pasta with zucchini noodles (zoodles), spaghetti squash, or shirataki noodles.
   - **Potatoes:** Use cauliflower to make mashed "potatoes" or roasted cauliflower bites instead of starchy sides.
   - **Sugar:** Substitute sugar with keto-friendly sweeteners like stevia, erythritol, or monk fruit.

2. **Plan Your Meals**

Effective meal planning is key to succeeding on the Keto Diet. Focus on meals that include healthy fats (avocados, olive oil, nuts), moderate proteins (chicken, salmon, eggs), and low-carb vegetables (spinach, broccoli, cauliflower). You can also prepare Keto-friendly versions of your favorite dishes to avoid feeling deprived.

3. **Shop Smart**

When grocery shopping, focus on whole, unprocessed foods. Stick to the perimeter of the grocery store where fresh produce, meats, and dairy products are found. Avoid processed snacks, sugary beverages, and high-carb foods.

4. **Master Keto Cooking Techniques**

Cooking with fats is central to Keto cuisine. Master techniques like sautéing with olive oil or butter, roasting meats and vegetables, and incorporating flavorful, high-fat sauces (like Hollandaise or avocado-based dips). Cooking meals at home gives you complete control over ingredients and carb content.

Making Keto meals enjoyable for all members of the family and Overcoming Challenges.

As we have written before The Keto diet known for its low-carbohydrate and high-fat approach, has become a popular lifestyle choice for many looking to improve their health and lose weight. However, adapting to this diet can be challenging, especially when trying to cater to the whole family. This article will provide practical tips and techniques to help you successfully incorporate the Keto diet into your family's lifestyle, ensuring it's enjoyable and sustainable for everyone.

Understanding the Keto Diet Basics

Before diving into meal preparation and family adaptation, it's essential to understand the Keto diet's fundamental principles:

Fats: 70-80% of your daily caloric intake should come from fats.
Proteins: 15-20% of your daily intake should be proteins.
Carbohydrates: Only 5-10% of your daily calories should come from carbohydrates.

The goal is to enter a state of ketosis, where the body burns fat for energy instead of carbohydrates.

Making Keto Meals Family-Friendly

1. **Start with Familiar Foods:** Introduce the Keto diet through familiar dishes that are already low-carb or can be easily adjusted. For example, replace regular pizza crust with a cauliflower crust and use zucchini noodles instead of pasta.
2. **Involve Everyone in Meal Planning:** Get input from all family members on what Keto-friendly dishes they'd enjoy. This inclusion can make the transition easier and more enjoyable for everyone.
3. **Creative Substitutions:** Use substitutions to recreate favorite meals. Almond and coconut flours are excellent for baking, and mashed cauliflower can stand in for mashed potatoes.
4. **Focus on Quality Fats:** Incorporate healthy fats like avocados, nuts, seeds, and olive oil into meals. These not only boost flavor but also increase satiety, which can be crucial for kids and active family members.

Tips for Success on the Keto Diet

- **Meal Prep:** Spend time each week preparing Keto meals and snacks. This helps avoid the temptation of non-Keto foods during busy times.
- **Educate Your Family:** Teach your family because certain foods are better on the Keto diet. Understanding the health benefits can make it easier for them to accept new eating habits.
- **Keep It Varied:** Ensure a variety of foods to keep meals interesting. Try new recipes regularly to discover new favorites.

Overcoming Challenges

- **Handling Cravings:** Keep Keto-friendly snacks available, such as cheese, nuts, and seeds, to handle cravings. Gradually, the high fat intake should help reduce cravings.
- **Dealing with Social Settings:** Prepare by eating beforehand or bringing Keto-friendly dishes to share. This way, you'll ensure there's something you can enjoy without feeling left out.
- **Monitoring Progress:** Keep track of your family's health and satisfaction levels and be willing to adjust the diet as needed. Not every family member may respond the same way to Keto, so it's important to remain flexible and responsive to their needs.

Making Keto Enjoyable

- **Theme Nights:** Try theme nights like "Keto Italian" or "Mexican Keto Night" to keep meals exciting and look forward to trying new things.
- **Cook Together:** Make meal preparation a family activity. This can help children learn about healthy eating and cooking skills.
- **Reward Improvements:** Celebrate milestones and improvements in health or weight goals. This can motivate continued adherence to the diet.

Successfully integrating the Keto diet into your family's lifestyle requires understanding, creativity, and flexibility. By focusing on familiar foods, involving everyone in the meal planning process, and educating your family on the benefits of Keto, you can make this diet not only manageable but also enjoyable for everyone. Remember, the goal of Keto is not just weight loss—it's about leading a healthier, more energetic life that your whole family can share.

CHAPTER 2

30-DAY MEAL PLAN

DAY	BREAKFAST	LUNCH	SNACK/DESSERT	DINNER
1	Keto Smoked Salmon and Cream Cheese Omelette -16p	Keto Caesar Salad with Chicken -29p	Coconut Chocolate Truffles-65p	Keto Chicken Parmesan-40p and Tomato Basil Marinara Sauce-71p
2	Chia Seed Pudding with Coconut-18p	Avocado Shrimp Salad -29p and Lemon Tahini Dressing-70p	Chocolate Chip Cookies -60p	Low-Carb Beef Stroganoff -41p
3	Almond Flour Waffles-18p	Turkey Bacon Ranch Wrap-31p and Cilantro Lime Dressing-69p	Almond Butter Brownies-61p	Seared Salmon with Creamy Dill Sauce-43p
4	Keto Avocado Toast on Cloud Bread-19p	Cauliflower Fried Rice-31p	Lemon Curd Tart-61p	Creamy Tuscan Garlic Chicken-43p
5	Bacon and Egg Cups-19p	Beef Taco Salad-32p and Keto Barbecue Sauce-69p	Baked Avocado Fries-58p and Buffalo Sauce-71p	Zucchini Lasagna-42p and Tomato Basil Marinara Sauce-71p
6	Keto Cream Cheese Pancakes-23p	Tuna Nicoise Salad-30p and Lemon Tahini Dressing-70p	Keto Blueberry Muffins -62p	Pork Chops with Mushroom Gravy-45p
7	Creamy Avocado Keto Smoothie-24p	Keto Sushi Rolls -35p	Coconut Bars-61p	Lemon Garlic Butter Steak-44p
8	Fried Egg with Broccoli and Cheese-17p	Spinach and Goat Cheese Stuffed Chicken-33p and Pesto Sauce-72p	Salmon and Cream Cheese Bites-57p	Keto Shepherd's Pie-44p
9	Keto Mushroom and Swiss Omelette-17p	Zucchini Noodle Caprese-34p and Pesto Sauce-72p	Keto Key Lime Pie-65p	Thai Coconut Curry Shrimp-41p
10	Keto Zucchini Fritters-21p and Hollandaise Sauce -72p	Pulled Pork with Cabbage Slaw-35p and Keto Barbecue Sauce-69p	Cheese and Herb Stuffed Mushrooms-54p	Eggplant and Beef Layered Casserole-46p and Tomato Basil Marinara Sauce-71p
11	Low-Carb Berry Porridge -24p	Creamy Tomato Basil Soup-36p and Keto Bagels -23p	Keto Tiramisu-63p	Baked Tilapia with Lemon Butter -47p
12	Ham and Cheese Keto Muffins-22p	Sausage and Peppers Skillet-31p	Pumpkin Spice Latte Cupcakes-64p	Cauliflower Crust Pizza with Mozzarella and Pepperoni-48p
13	Keto Greek Yogurt with Keto Granola-20p	Pork Lettuce Wraps -33p and Cilantro Lime Dressing-69p	Coconut Chocolate Truffles-65p	Keto Meatloaf-42p and Keto Gravy-70p
14	Egg Salad in Lettuce Cups -21p	Cobb Salad with Keto Vinaigrette-32p	Bacon-Wrapped Asparagus-56p	Spaghetti Squash Carbonara-45p
15	Keto Pesto Egg Muffins -25p	Creamy Chicken and Asparagus-36p	Almond Butter Brownies -61p	Roast Turkey with Low -Carb Gravy-49p
16	Almond Butter and Blueberry Smoothie-26p	Cheesy Taco Skillet-34p	Salted Caramel Pudding -66p	Cod in Creamy Red Roasted Pepper Sauce -49p

DAY	BREAKFAST	LUNCH	SNACK/DESSERT	DINNER
17	Keto Power Breakfast Bowl-25p	Turkey Bacon Ranch Wrap-31p and Buffalo Sauce-71p	Coconut Bars-61p	Keto Chicken Cacciatore -46p
18	Baked Avocado Eggs-16p	Keto Reuben Sandwich -38p	Snickerdoodle Cream Cookies-66p	Fried Broccoli with Garlic and Shrimp-47p
19	Keto Bagels-23p and Pesto Sause-72p	Cauliflower Fried Rice-31p	Blackberry Cobbler-67p	Pan-Seared Duck Breast with Red Wine Sauce-50p
20	Spinach and Mushroom Quiche-27p	Avocado Shrimp Salad-29p and Cilantro Lime Dressing-69p	Cauliflower Hummus -54p	Garlic Parmesan Chicken Wings-50p
21	Keto Eggs Benedict-22p and Hollandaise Sauce -72p	Tuna Nicoise Salad-30p and Lemon Tahini Dressing-70p	Cheese and Herb Stuffed Mushrooms-54p	Lamb Chops with Mint Pesto-48p
22	Keto Cream Cheese Pancakes-23p	Pulled Pork with Cabbage Slaw-35p and Keto Barbecue Sauce-69p	Pumpkin Spice Latte Cupcakes-64p	Low-Carb Beef Stroganoff -41p
23	Creamy Avocado Keto Smoothie-24p	Beef Taco Salad -32p and Buffalo Sauce-71p	Keto Blondies-64p	Keto Shepherd's Pie-44p
24	Keto Zucchini and Egg Breakfast Bowl-26p	Cream of Mushroom Soup-37p and Keto Bagels-23p	Garlic Cheese Bread Sticks-56p	Baked Tilapia with Lemon Butter -47p
25	Caramel Pecan Porridge -27p	Keto Sushi Rolls-35p	Bacon-Wrapped Asparagus-56p	Keto Meatloaf-42p and Keto Gravy-70p
26	Chia Seed Pudding with Coconut-18p	Cobb Salad with Keto Vinaigrette-32p	Coconut Chocolate Truffles-65p	Zucchini Lasagna-42p and Tomato Basil Marinara Sauce-71p
27	Fried Egg with Broccoli and Cheese-17p	Pork Lettuce Wraps-33p and Cilantro Lime Dressing-69p	Salted Caramel Pudding -66p	Lemon Garlic Butter Steak -44p
28	Ham and Cheese Keto Muffins-22p	Creamy Chicken and Asparagus-36p	Snickerdoodle Cream Cookies-66p	Seared Salmon with Creamy Dill Sauce-43p
29	Keto Mushroom and Swiss Omelette-17p	Sausage and Peppers Skillet-31p	Bacon Avocado Bombs -53p	Eggplant and Beef Layered Casserole-46p and Tomato Basil Marinara Sauce-71p
30	Almond Flour Waffles-18p	Spinach and Goat Cheese Stuffed Chicken-33p and Pesto Sauce-72p	Cauliflower Hummus -54p	Thai Coconut Curry Shrimp-41p

Note:

Welcome to your 30-Day Keto Meal Plan, meticulously crafted to introduce you to the rich and satisfying world of ketogenic cuisine. This plan is designed not only to guide you but to delight you with meals that are as nourishing as they are delectable. Each recipe embraces the core principles of the keto diet—low in carbohydrates, high in healthy fats, and moderate in protein—to help you achieve and maintain a state of ketosis.

Please be aware that the calorie may vary based on the specific ingredients and portion sizes you choose. Each day's menu is balanced to ensure you receive a comprehensive range of nutrients while adhering to keto guidelines. If the estimated calorie counts do not align with your personal dietary goals, feel free to adjust portion sizes or substitute ingredients to better suit your needs.

This meal plan is flexible; it's meant to be tailored to your preferences and nutritional requirements. As you embark on this journey, embrace the variety of flavors and the wholesome ingredients that make the keto diet both enjoyable and sustainable. Savor every meal, and let each bite be a step toward a healthier, more energized you.

Enjoy your culinary adventure into keto living!

BREAKFASTS

Energizing starts to the day with easy recipes

Keto Smoked Salmon and Cream Cheese Omelette

 Yield: 1 serving   **Preparation Time:** 5 minutes   **Cooking Time:** 5 minutes

Ingredients:

- 2 large eggs
- 2 tablespoons heavy cream
- 1 ounce smoked salmon, sliced
- 1 ounce cream cheese, cut into small pieces
- 1 tablespoon chives, finely chopped
- 1 tablespoon butter
- Salt and pepper, to taste
- 1 teaspoon capers (for garnish)
- 1 tablespoon red onion, finely chopped (for garnish)
- A few sprigs of dill (for garnish)

Instructions:

1. Prepare the Egg Mixture. In a mixing bowl, whisk together the eggs, heavy cream, salt, and pepper until well blended.
2. Cook the Omelette. Melt the butter in a non-stick skillet over medium heat. Pour the egg mixture into the skillet. Tilt the pan to ensure the eggs evenly coat the surface. As the eggs begin to set, gently place the smoked salmon slices and cream cheese pieces over half of the omelette. Sprinkle with chives. Carefully fold the other half of the omelette over the filled side. Let it cook for another minute to allow the cream cheese to soften.
3. Garnish and Serve. Transfer the omelette to a plate. If desired, top with capers, red onion, and dill for additional flavor and a visual appeal. Serve immediately while hot.

Baked Avocado Eggs

 Yield: 2 servings (2 avocado halves per serving) 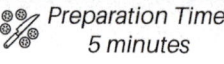 **Preparation Time:** 5 minutes   **Cooking Time:** 15 minutes

Ingredients:

- 2 large ripe avocados
- 4 large eggs
- Salt and black pepper, to taste
- 1/4 teaspoon paprika (optional)
- 2 tablespoons chopped chives or green onions, for garnish
- 2 tablespoons crumbled bacon or cooked chorizo (optional, for added flavor)
- A sprinkle of grated Parmesan or cheddar cheese
- A few dashes of hot sauce or salsa

Instructions:

1. Preheat the oven to 425°F (220°C). Prepare Avocados: Cut the avocados in half and remove the pits. Scoop out a little more avocado flesh to make enough room for an egg in each half. Place the avocado halves in a baking dish to keep them stable.
2. Crack an egg into each avocado half. It's okay if some of the egg white spills over. Season with salt and black pepper. Sprinkle with paprika, and add cheese, hot sauce, or salsa if using.
3. Bake: Place the avocados in the preheated oven and bake for about 15 minutes, or until the egg whites are set and yolks are cooked to your desired doneness.
4. Garnish and Serve. Remove from the oven and sprinkle with chopped chives, green onions, and optional bacon or chorizo. Enjoy warm as a nutritious and satisfying keto breakfast or brunch.

Nutritional Information (Per Serving):

Calories: 400 kcal | Protein: 20 g | Carbohydrates: 3 g | Fats: 34 g | Cholesterol: 375 mg | Sodium: 580 mg | Potassium: 200 mg

Nutritional Information (Per Serving):

Calories: 480 kcal | Protein: 18 g | Carbohydrates: 12 g | Fats: 42 g | Cholesterol: 370 mg | Sodium: 400 mg | Potassium: 1060 mg

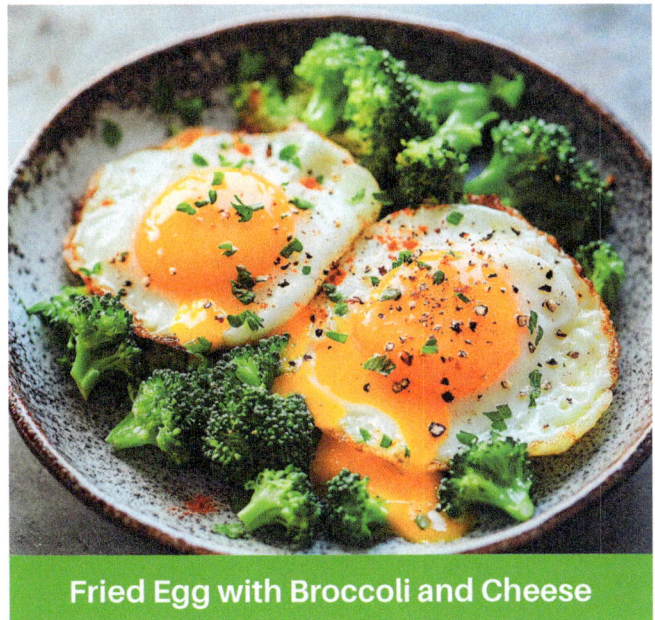

Fried Egg with Broccoli and Cheese

Yield: 2 serving | Preparation Time: 5 minutes | Cooking Time: 10 minutes

Ingredients:

- 4 large eggs
- 1 cup broccoli florets, chopped into small bite-sized pieces
- 1/2 cup shredded cheddar cheese
- 2 tbsp butter (grass-fed, unsalted)
- 1 tbsp olive oil
- Salt and pepper, to taste
- 1/2 tsp smoked paprika (optional, for a smoky kick)
- Fresh parsley or chives, chopped for garnish (optional)

Instructions:

1. Wash and chop the broccoli into small florets to ensure they cook evenly. Shred the cheese if it isn't already prepared.
2. Heat 1 tablespoon of butter and 1 tablespoon of olive oil in a large skillet over medium heat. Add the chopped broccoli and cook for 4-5 minutes until it becomes tender and slightly crispy on the edges. Season the broccoli with salt, pepper. Stir occasionally to ensure even cooking. Once cooked, push the broccoli to one side of the skillet.
3. Add the remaining tablespoon of butter to the skillet. Once melted, crack the eggs into the pan next to the broccoli, making sure not to break the yolks. Cook the eggs to your preference. For sunny-side-up eggs, cook for about 3-4 minutes until the whites are set but the yolks remain runny. For over-easy eggs, flip them gently after 2-3 minutes and cook for an additional 1-2 minutes.
4. Once the eggs are almost done cooking, sprinkle the shredded cheese evenly over the broccoli and eggs. Cover the skillet with a lid and allow the cheese to melt for about 1 minute.
5. Remove the skillet from heat. Plate the eggs and broccoli, ensuring the melted cheese is spread evenly. Garnish with freshly chopped parsley or chives if desired.

Nutritional Information (Per Serving):

Calories: 380 kcal | Protein: 18g | Carbohydrates: 5g | Fat: 32g | Cholesterol: 370mg | Sodium: 480mg | Potassium: 380mg

Keto Mushroom and Swiss Omelette

Yield: 1 serving | Preparation Time: 5 minutes | Cooking Time: 10 minutes

Ingredients:

- 3 large eggs
- 1 tablespoon heavy cream (or unsweetened almond milk for a lighter option)
- 1/2 cup mushrooms, sliced
- 1/4 cup Swiss cheese, shredded
- 2 tablespoons butter or olive oil
- Salt and pepper, to taste

Instructions:

1. Clean and slice mushrooms: Wash the mushrooms thoroughly and slice them evenly. Chop herbs and onions: If using, chop the chives, parsley, and onions finely.
2. Heat the skillet: In a non-stick skillet, heat 1 tablespoon of butter or olive oil over medium heat. Sauté mushrooms and onions: Add the mushrooms and onions to the skillet. Cook for about 5 minutes or until the mushrooms are golden and the onions are translucent. Season with garlic powder, salt, and pepper during the last minute.
3. Make the Omelette: In a bowl, whisk the eggs with heavy cream, salt, and pepper until well combined. Cook the omelette: In the same skillet, add another tablespoon of butter or oil and pour in the egg mixture. Cook over medium heat. Add fillings: As the eggs begin to set, sprinkle the sautéed mushrooms and shredded Swiss cheese evenly over one half of the omelette. Fold the omelette: Carefully fold the other half of the omelette over the filled half. Let it cook for another 2-3 minutes to ensure the cheese melts.
4. Slide the omelette onto a plate, and garnish with chopped chives and parsley if desired. Serve hot.

Nutritional Information (Per Serving):

Calories: 450 kcal | Protein: 31 g | Carbohydrates: 5 g | Fats: 35 g | Cholesterol: 550 mg | Sodium: 400 mg | Potassium: 300 mg

Almond Flour Waffles

 Yield:
2 servings
(4 waffles)

 Preparation Time:
5 minutes

 Cooking Time:
10 minutes

Ingredients:

- 1 cup almond flour
- 2 large eggs
- 1/4 cup heavy cream (or unsweetened almond milk for a lighter option)
- 2 tablespoons unsalted butter, melted
- 1 tablespoon erythritol (or any other keto-friendly sweetener)
- 1 teaspoon vanilla extract
- 1/2 teaspoon baking powder
- Pinch of salt
- Whipped cream (sugar-free)
- Fresh berries (such as raspberries or blueberries)
- Sugar-free maple syrup

Instructions:

1. Combine Dry Ingredients: In a large bowl, mix the almond flour, baking powder, erythritol, salt, and optional cinnamon until well combined. Add Wet Ingredients: Beat in the eggs, heavy cream, melted butter, and vanilla extract until the batter is smooth. If using, fold in sugar-free chocolate chips.
2. Preheat Your Waffle Iron: Heat your waffle iron according to the manufacturer's instructions and grease it lightly with butter or non-stick spray to prevent sticking. Bake the Waffles: Pour enough batter to cover the center of the waffle iron, not filling it completely to allow for expansion. Close the lid and cook for about 3-5 minutes, or until the waffle is golden and crisp. Repeat: Continue with the remaining batter, greasing the iron as needed between batches.
3. Serving: Serve the waffles hot from the waffle iron. Garnish with a dollop of sugar-free whipped cream, fresh berries, and a drizzle of sugar-free maple syrup if desired.

Nutritional Information (Per Serving):

Calories: 580 kcal | Protein: 20 g | Carbohydrates: 12 g
Fats: 50 g | Cholesterol: 220 mg | Sodium: 300 mg
Potassium: 200 mg

Chia Seed Pudding with Coconut

Yield:
2 servings

Preparation Time:
10 minutes (plus at least 4 hours chilling time)

Cooking Time:
0 minutes

Ingredients:

- 1/4 cup chia seeds
- 1 cup canned coconut milk (full-fat)
- 1/2 cup unsweetened almond milk
- 2 tablespoons erythritol (or any keto-friendly sweetener)
- 1 teaspoon vanilla extract
- 1/4 teaspoon cinnamon (optional for flavor)
- Pinch of salt
- Unsweetened shredded coconut
- Fresh berries such as raspberries or blueberries
- Chopped nuts (like almonds or pecans)

Instructions:

1. Combine Liquids: In a mixing bowl or large measuring cup, whisk together the coconut milk, almond milk, vanilla extract, and erythritol until the sweetener is completely dissolved. Add Chia Seeds: Stir in the chia seeds, cinnamon, and a pinch of salt until well combined.
2. Refrigerate: Pour the mixture into two serving glasses or a sealed container. Let it sit for about 10 minutes, then stir again to prevent the chia seeds from clumping together. Refrigerate Again: Cover and refrigerate for at least 4 hours, ideally overnight, until it achieves a pudding-like consistency.
3. Garnish and Serve: Once set, stir the pudding once more, and if it's too thick, adjust the consistency by adding a little more almond milk. Top with unsweetened shredded coconut, fresh berries, and chopped nuts before serving.

Nutritional Information (Per Serving):

Calories: 350 kcal | Protein: 6 g | Carbohydrates: 10 g
Fats: 29 g | Cholesterol: 0 mg | Sodium: 55 mg
Potassium: 300 mg

Keto Avocado Toast on Cloud Bread

 Yield:
2 serving 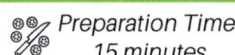 Preparation Time:
15 minutes Cooking Time:
30 minutes

Ingredients:

For the Cloud Bread:
- 3 large eggs, separated
- 3 tablespoons cream cheese, softened
- 1/4 teaspoon cream of tartar
- 1 tablespoon erythritol (optional, for a slightly sweet flavor)

For the Topping:
- 1 large avocado

- 1 tablespoon lime juice
- Salt and pepper, to taste
- 1/2 teaspoon red pepper flakes (optional)
- 2 tablespoons feta cheese, crumbled (optional)
- 2 teaspoons fresh cilantro, chopped (optional)

Instructions:

1. Make the Cloud Bread. Preheat the oven to 300°F (150°C). Line a baking sheet with parchment paper. In a large bowl, beat the egg whites with the cream of tartar until stiff peaks form. In another bowl, mix the egg yolks, cream cheese, and optional erythritol until smooth. Gently fold the yolk mixture into the beaten egg whites, taking care not to deflate the mixture. Spoon the mixture onto the prepared baking sheet, forming 4 even rounds. Bake for about 25-30 minutes or until golden brown. Remove and let cool.
2. Prepare Avocado Topping. In a bowl, mash the avocado with lime juice, salt, and pepper. Mix in red pepper flakes, feta cheese, and cilantro if using.
3. Assemble and Serve. Spread the mashed avocado evenly over the cloud bread slices. Enjoy your Keto Avocado Toast fresh for the best texture and flavor.

Nutritional Information (Per Serving):

Calories: 320 kcal | Protein: 9 g | Carbohydrates: 8 g
Fats: 27 g | Cholesterol: 165 mg | Sodium: 200 mg
Potassium: 500 mg

Bacon and Egg Cups

 Yield:
6 servings
(12 egg cups) Preparation Time:
10 minutes Cooking Time:
20 minutes

Ingredients:

- 12 slices of bacon
- 12 large eggs
- 1/2 cup shredded cheddar cheese
- 1/4 cup finely chopped green onions
- Salt and pepper, to taste
- Fresh herbs such as parsley or chives, chopped
- Sour cream or avocado slices

Instructions:

1. Prepare the Bacon. Preheat the oven to 375°F (190°C). Arrange the bacon slices on a baking sheet lined with parchment paper. Bake for 10 minutes, just until the bacon is partially cooked but still pliable. Remove from the oven and let cool slightly.
2. Assemble the Egg Cups. Grease a 12-cup muffin tin with butter or cooking spray. Wrap one slice of bacon around the inside of each muffin cup. Sprinkle a bit of shredded cheese into each bacon-lined cup. Season with salt, pepper, garlic powder, and paprika if using.
3. Add the Eggs. Carefully crack an egg into each bacon and cheese-lined cup. The egg should fit snugly inside the bacon wrap. Sprinkle the chopped green onions over the eggs.
4. Bake the Egg Cups. Return the muffin tin to the oven and bake at 375°F (190°C) for 12-15 minutes, or until the egg whites are set and the yolks are cooked to your liking.
5. Serve. Let the bacon and egg cups cool in the pan for a few minutes, then carefully remove them using a spoon or a butter knife. Garnish with fresh herbs, sour cream, or avocado slices if desired.

Nutritional Information (Per Serving):

Calories: 380 kcal | Protein: 26 g | Carbohydrates: 2 g
Fats: 30 g | Cholesterol: 430 mg | Sodium: 620 mg
Potassium: 250 mg

Keto Breakfast Burrito with Cauliflower Wrap

🍽 Yield: 2 serving ✹ Preparation Time: 15 minutes 🍲 Cooking Time: 15 minutes

Keto Greek Yogurt with Keto Granola

🍽 Yield: 2 servings ✹ Preparation Time: 10 minutes 🍲 Cooking Time: 20 minutes *(for granola)*

Ingredients:

For the Cauliflower Wrap:
- 2 cups cauliflower rice
- 2 large eggs
- 1/4 cup almond flour
- 1/2 teaspoon garlic powder
- Salt and pepper, to taste

For the Filling:
- 4 large eggs
- 1/2 cup shredded cheddar cheese

- 4 slices bacon, cooked and crumbled
- 1/4 cup chopped bell peppers
- 1/4 cup chopped onions
- 2 tablespoons chopped cilantro (optional)
- 1/2 avocado, sliced (optional for garnish)
- Sour cream (optional for serving)

Instructions:

1. Heat a skillet over medium heat. Add the cauliflower rice and cook for 5-7 minutes until tender and moisture has evaporated. Let it cool slightly. In a mixing bowl, combine the cooked cauliflower rice, eggs, almond flour, garlic powder, salt, and pepper. Mix until well combined. Heat a non-stick skillet over medium heat. Scoop half of the cauliflower mixture onto the skillet, spreading it into a thin, round shape. Cook for 3-4 minutes per side until firm and golden. Repeat with the remaining mixture.
2. Whisk the eggs in a bowl. In the same skillet, sauté onions and bell peppers until soft. Add the scrambled eggs and cook, stirring until the eggs are set. Stir in the cheddar cheese and crumbled bacon, cooking until the cheese is melted. Remove from heat and stir in the cilantro.
3. Divide the filling between the two cauliflower wraps. Add avocado slices if using. Fold the sides of the wraps over the filling, then roll tightly to form a burrito.
4. Serve the burritos immediately, garnished with sour cream and salsa if desired.

Ingredients:

For the Keto Granola:
- 1 cup almonds, roughly chopped
- 1/2 cup pecans, roughly chopped
- 1/4 cup sunflower seeds
- 1/4 cup pumpkin seeds
- 2 tablespoons unsweetened coconut flakes
- 2 tablespoons flaxseeds
- 1/4 cup erythritol (or another keto-friendly sweetener)
- 1/4 cup melted coconut oil
- 1 teaspoon vanilla extract
- 1/2 teaspoon cinnamon
- Pinch of salt

For the Greek Yogurt:
- 1 cup full-fat Greek yogurt

Optional for added flavor:
- Fresh berries
- A few drops of stevia (if additional sweetness is desired)
- 1/4 teaspoon lemon zest (for garnish)

Instructions:

1. Preheat the oven to 300°F (150°C) and line a baking sheet with parchment paper. In a bowl, combine the almonds, pecans, sunflower seeds, pumpkin seeds, coconut flakes, and flaxseeds. Stir in the melted coconut oil, erythritol, vanilla extract, cinnamon, and a pinch of salt until everything is well coated. Spread the mixture evenly on the prepared baking sheet. Bake for about 20 minutes, stirring halfway through, until the granola is lightly golden and fragrant. Remove from the oven and let cool completely; it will crisp up as it cools.
2. Divide the Greek yogurt between two bowls. If additional sweetness is desired, mix a few drops of stevia into the yogurt before serving. Top each bowl of yogurt with a generous amount of the cooled keto granola. Optionally, add fresh berries and a sprinkle of lemon zest for enhanced flavor and visual appeal.
3. Enjoy this wholesome and satisfying keto-friendly breakfast immediately for the best texture and freshness of the granola.

Nutritional Information (Per Serving):

Calories: 560 kcal | Protein: 32 g | Carbohydrates: 12 g
Fats: 42 g | Cholesterol: 490 mg | Sodium: 720 mg
Potassium: 600 mg

Nutritional Information (Per Serving):

Calories: 650 kcal | Protein: 22 g | Carbohydrates: 20 g
Fats: 55 g | Cholesterol: 30 mg | Sodium: 80 mg
Potassium: 400 mg

Keto Zucchini Fritters

 Yield:
4 servings
(8 fritters)

Preparation Time:
15 minutes

Cooking Time:
10 minutes

Ingredients:

- 2 medium zucchini, grated (about 2 cups)
- 1/4 cup almond flour
- 1/4 cup grated Parmesan cheese
- 2 large eggs
- 2 cloves garlic, minced
- 1/2 teaspoon salt
- 1/4 teaspoon black pepper
- 2 tablespoons olive oil or avocado oil for frying
- Sour cream or Greek yogurt (keto-friendly)
- Lemon wedges

Instructions:

1. Prepare the Zucchini. Drain Zucchini: Place the grated zucchini in a colander, sprinkle with a little salt, and let it sit for 10 minutes to draw out moisture. Squeeze out the excess liquid using a clean kitchen towel or cheesecloth.
2. Make the Fritter Mixture. In a large bowl, mix the drained zucchini, almond flour, Parmesan cheese, eggs, garlic, salt, pepper until well combined.
3. Cook the Fritters. In a large skillet, heat the olive oil or avocado oil over medium heat. Scoop heaping tablespoons of the zucchini mixture into the hot oil, flattening them slightly with the back of the spoon to form rounds. Fry for about 2-3 minutes on each side or until golden brown and crispy. Transfer the fritters to a paper towel-lined plate to remove excess oil.
4. Serve the zucchini fritters hot with a side of sour cream or Greek yogurt and lemon wedges for extra flavor.

Nutritional Information (Per Serving):

Calories: 210 kcal | Protein: 9 g | Carbohydrates: 6 g
Fats: 17 g | Cholesterol: 95 mg | Sodium: 370 mg
Potassium: 340 mg

Egg Salad in Lettuce Cups

 Yield:
2 serving

Preparation Time:
10 minutes

Cooking Time:
10 minutes

Ingredients:

- 4 large eggs
- 1/4 cup mayonnaise (preferably avocado oil-based)
- 1 tablespoon Dijon mustard
- 1/4 cup celery, finely chopped
- 2 tablespoons red onion, finely chopped
- Salt and pepper, to taste
- 6 large lettuce leaves (Romaine or Butter lettuce work well)
- Paprika, for sprinkling
- 2 tablespoons chives, chopped

Instructions:

1. Cook the Eggs. Place eggs in a saucepan and cover with water. Bring to a boil, then cover, turn off the heat, and let sit for 10 minutes. After 10 minutes, place eggs in cold water to cool. Once cooled, peel the eggs and roughly chop them into bite-sized pieces.
2. Prepare the Egg Salad. In a bowl, combine the chopped eggs, mayonnaise, Dijon mustard, celery, and red onion. Mix gently until well combined. Season with salt and pepper to taste.
3. Assemble the Lettuce Cups. Wash and dry the lettuce leaves. Choose leaves that
4. Serve. Sprinkle each filled lettuce cup with a bit of paprika and chopped chives for garnish. Serve immediately.

Nutritional Information (Per Serving):

Calories: 350 kcal | Protein: 14 g | Carbohydrates: 4 g
Fats: 30 g | Cholesterol: 390 mg | Sodium: 450 mg
Potassium: 300 mg

Ham and Cheese Muffins

Yield: 6 servings (12 muffins) | **Preparation Time:** 10 minutes | **Cooking Time:** 20 minutes

Ingredients:

- 1 1/2 cups almond flour
- 1/4 cup coconut flour
- 1 teaspoon baking powder
- 1/2 teaspoon salt
- 1/4 teaspoon black pepper
- 6 large eggs
- 1/2 cup sour cream
- 1/4 cup olive oil
- 1 cup cheddar cheese, shredded
- 1 cup cooked ham, finely diced
- 1/4 cup green onions, chopped
- Chopped parsley or chives

Instructions:

1. Preheat the oven to 350°F (175°C). Grease a 12-cup muffin tin or line with silicone muffin liners. In a large bowl, combine the almond flour, coconut flour, baking powder, salt, and black pepper.
2. In another bowl, whisk the eggs, sour cream, and olive oil until smooth. Add Cheeses and Ham: Stir in the shredded cheese, diced ham, and green onions.
3. Make the Muffin Batter. Add the wet ingredients to the dry ingredients and stir until just combined.
4. Bake the Muffins. Fill Muffin Cups: Spoon the batter into the prepared muffin tin, filling each cup about 3/4 full. Sprinkle additional cheese on top if desired. Place in the oven and bake for 18-20 minutes, or until the tops are golden and a toothpick inserted into the center of a muffin comes out clean.
5. Cooling and Serving. Allow the muffins to cool in the pan for 5 minutes, then transfer to a wire rack to cool completely. Garnish with chopped parsley or chives if desired.

Nutritional Information (Per Serving):

Calories: 450 kcal | Protein: 20 g | Carbohydrates: 9 g
Fats: 37 g | Cholesterol: 230 mg | Sodium: 600 mg
Potassium: 200 mg

Keto Eggs Benedict

Yield: 2 servings | **Preparation Time:** 15 minutes | **Cooking Time:** 10 minutes

Ingredients:

For the English Muffins:
- 1/2 cup almond flour
- 1 tablespoon coconut flour
- 1/2 teaspoon baking powder
- 1/4 teaspoon salt
- 2 tablespoons unsalted butter, melted
- 2 large eggs

For the Hollandaise Sauce:
- 2 large egg yolks
- 1 tablespoon lemon juice
- 1/2 teaspoon Dijon mustard
- 1/4 cup unsalted butter, melted
- Salt and cayenne pepper, to taste

For the Eggs Benedict:
- 4 large eggs
- 4 slices of cooked ham or bacon

Instructions:

1. Make the English Muffins: Preheat the oven to 350°F (175°C). Mix almond flour, coconut flour, baking powder, and salt in a bowl. Whisk in the melted butter and eggs until smooth. Divide the batter into 4 equal portions on a baking sheet lined with parchment paper. Bake for 12-15 minutes or until golden brown. Let them cool slightly and slice horizontally.
2. Prepare the Hollandaise Sauce: In a heatproof bowl, whisk together egg yolks, lemon juice, and Dijon mustard. Place the bowl over a pot of simmering water (double boiler method), ensuring the water does not touch the bottom of the bowl. Whisk vigorously while slowly drizzling in the melted butter until the sauce thickens. Remove from heat and season with salt and cayenne pepper. Keep warm.
3. Poach the Eggs: Bring a pot of water to a gentle simmer and add a splash of vinegar. Crack each egg into a small cup and gently pour it into the simmering water. Cook for 3-4 minutes until the whites are set but the yolks remain runny. Remove with a slotted spoon and drain on a kitchen towel.
4. Assemble the Eggs Benedict: Place a slice of ham or bacon on each half of the English muffin. Top with a poached egg. Drizzle generously with Hollandaise sauce.

Nutritional Information (Per Serving):

Calories: 623 kcal | Protein: 25 g | Carbohydrates: 7 g
Fat: 56 g | Fiber: 3 g | Cholesterol: 685 mg | Sodium: 912 mg | Potassium: 300 mg

Keto Bagels

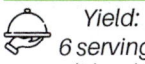 **Yield:**
6 servings
(6 bagels)

 Preparation Time:
15 minutes

Cooking Time:
12-15 minutes

Ingredients:

- 1 1/2 cups almond flour
- 1 tablespoon coconut flour
- 2 teaspoons baking powder
- 2 1/2 cups shredded mozzarella cheese
- 2 ounces cream cheese
- 2 large eggs

Optional for topping:
- Sesame seeds
- Poppy seeds
- Dried garlic flakes
- Dried onion flakes
- Coarse salt

Instructions:

1. Prepare the Dough. Preheat the oven to 400°F (200°C). Line a baking sheet with parchment paper. In a bowl, combine the almond flour, coconut flour, baking powder. In a separate microwave-safe bowl, combine the mozzarella and cream cheese. Microwave on high for about 90 seconds, stirring halfway through, until fully melted and easy to stir. Stir the dry ingredients into the melted cheese mixture. Add the eggs and mix until a smooth dough forms. You may need to knead with your hands to fully incorporate the eggs.
2. Shape the Bagels. Divide the dough into 6 equal portions. Roll each portion into a ball, then press your finger through the center to form a ring. Arrange the bagels on the prepared baking sheet. Ensure they have space to expand slightly.
3. Add Toppings. Apply Egg Wash (optional for a glossy finish): Beat an additional egg and brush over the top of each bagel. Add sesame seeds, poppy seeds, dried garlic, dried onion, or coarse salt as desired.
4. Bake: Place in the oven and bake for 12-15 minutes, or until golden brown.
5. Serving. Allow the bagels to cool on the baking sheet for 10 minutes, then transfer to a wire rack to cool completely.

Nutritional Information (Per Serving):

Calories: 350 kcal | Protein: 21 g | Carbohydrates: 8 g
Fats: 27 g | Cholesterol: 120 mg | Sodium: 450 mg
Potassium: 100 mg

Keto Cream Cheese Pancakes

Yield:
2 servings
(6 pancakes)

Preparation Time:
5 minutes

Cooking Time:
10 minutes

Ingredients:

- 2 ounces cream cheese, softened
- 2 large eggs
- 1 tablespoon coconut flour
- 1/2 teaspoon vanilla extract
- 1/2 teaspoon cinnamon (optional)
- 1 tablespoon erythritol (or other keto-friendly sweetener)
- Butter or coconut oil, for frying
- Fresh berries
- Whipped cream (sugar-free)
- Sugar-free syrup

Instructions:

1. Blend the Ingredients. In a blender, combine the cream cheese, eggs, coconut flour, vanilla extract, cinnamon, and erythritol. Blend until the mixture is smooth.
2. Cook the Pancakes. Heat a non-stick skillet over medium heat and add a little butter or coconut oil. Pour about 2 tablespoons of the batter per pancake into the hot skillet. Cook for 2-3 minutes on each side or until golden brown and easy to flip. Continue cooking all the pancakes, adding more butter or oil to the skillet as needed.
3. Serve. Serve the pancakes hot from the skillet. Top with sugar-free whipped cream, fresh berries, and sugar-free syrup if desired.

Nutritional Information (Per Serving):

Calories: 240 kcal | Protein: 10 g | Carbohydrates: 4 g
Fats: 20 g | Cholesterol: 215 mg | Sodium: 200 mg
Potassium: 150 mg

Creamy Avocado Keto Smoothie

 Yield: 2 servings　 **Preparation Time:** 5 minutes　**Cooking Time:** 0 minutes

Ingredients:

- 1 cup unsweetened almond milk
- 1/4 cup heavy cream
- 1/2 medium avocado
- 2 tablespoons almond butter
- 1 tablespoon flaxseed meal
- 1 tablespoon unsweetened cocoa powder
- 1 scoop protein powder (vanilla or unflavored, low-carb)
- Stevia or erythritol to taste

Optional for garnish:
- Whipped cream (sugar-free)
- A sprinkle of chia seeds

Instructions:

1. Prepare Ingredients: Have all ingredients ready. Ensure the avocado is ripe and scoop out the required amount.
2. Combine Ingredients in Blender: Add the almond milk, heavy cream, avocado, almond butter, flaxseed meal, cocoa powder, and protein powder to a blender. Blend on high speed until the mixture is completely smooth and creamy. Taste and adjust sweetness with stevia or erythritol as desired.
3. Serve: Pour the smoothie into a serving glass. If desired, top with a dollop of sugar-free whipped cream and a sprinkle of chia seeds for extra texture and nutrients.

Nutritional Information (Per Serving):

Calories: 340 kcal | Protein: 10 g | Carbohydrates: 8 g
Total Fat: 32 g | Cholesterol: 62 mg | Sodium: 110 mg
Potassium: 205 mg

Low-Carb Berry Porridge

 Yield: 2 servings　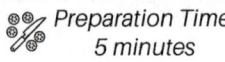 **Preparation Time:** 5 minutes　 **Cooking Time:** 10 minutes

Ingredients:

- 1/2 cup almond flour
- 1/4 cup ground flaxseed
- 2 tablespoons chia seeds
- 1 cup unsweetened almond milk
- 1/2 cup coconut cream
- 1/4 teaspoon cinnamon
- 1/2 cup mixed berries (raspberries, blueberries, strawberries)
- Sweetener to taste (erythritol, stevia, or monk fruit)

Optional for added flavor:
- 1/4 teaspoon vanilla extract
- Pinch of salt
- Optional for garnish:
- Additional berries
- A sprinkle of chopped nuts (almonds, pecans)
- Dollop of whipped cream (sugar-free)

Instructions:

1. Prepare the Porridge. In a medium saucepan, mix the almond flour, ground flaxseed, and chia seeds. Pour in the almond milk and coconut cream, stirring well to combine and ensure there are no lumps. Place the saucepan over medium heat. Bring the mixture to a simmer, stirring frequently to prevent sticking.
2. Add Flavors and Berries. Add the cinnamon, optional vanilla extract, and a pinch of salt. Sweeten to taste with your choice of keto-friendly sweetener. Add the mixed berries to the saucepan. Stir gently to combine and heat through, allowing the berries to release their juices and flavor the porridge.
3. Simmer and Serve. Allow the mixture to simmer for about 5-7 minutes, or until the porridge has thickened to your liking. Divide the porridge into bowls.
4. Garnish with additional berries, chopped nuts, and a dollop of whipped cream if desired. Enjoy your keto-friendly berry porridge warm for a comforting and satisfying meal.

Nutritional Information (Per Serving):

Calories: 400 kcal | Protein: 10 g | Carbohydrates: 15 g
Fats: 35 g | Cholesterol: 0 mg | Sodium: 80 mg
Potassium: 300 mg

Keto Power Breakfast Bowl

Yield: 2 servings | **Preparation Time:** 10 minutes | **Cooking Time:** 15 minutes

Ingredients:

- 4 large eggs
- 4 slices of bacon, chopped
- 1 cup fresh spinach
- 1/2 avocado, sliced
- 1/4 cup cherry tomatoes, halved
- 2 tablespoons olive oil or avocado oil
- 1/4 cup shredded cheddar cheese
- Salt and pepper, to taste
- 1/2 teaspoon crushed red pepper flakes
- 2 tablespoons sour cream
- 1 tablespoon chives, chopped

Instructions:

1. Cook the Bacon. In a large skillet, heat 1 tablespoon of oil over medium heat. Add the chopped bacon to the skillet and cook until crispy, about 5-7 minutes. Remove the bacon from the skillet and set aside on a paper towel-lined plate to drain.
2. Prepare the Eggs. In the same skillet, use the remaining bacon fat to cook the eggs. Crack the eggs into the skillet and gently scramble until fully cooked but still soft. Season with salt and pepper.
3. Assemble the Breakfast Bowl. In another pan, quickly sauté the spinach with the remaining tablespoon of oil just until wilted, about 1-2 minutes. Season with a pinch of salt. Divide the sautéed spinach between two bowls. Add the scrambled eggs and crispy bacon. Top each bowl with sliced avocado, halved cherry tomatoes, and shredded cheddar cheese.
4. Garnish and Serve. Sprinkle each bowl with crushed red pepper flakes, a dollop of sour cream, and chopped chives. Enjoy the breakfast bowls immediately while warm.

Nutritional Information (Per Serving):

Calories: 600 kcal | Protein: 30 g | Carbohydrates: 8 g
Fats: 50 g | Cholesterol: 390 mg | Sodium: 850 mg
Potassium: 400 mg

Keto Pesto Egg Muffins

Yield: 6 servings (12 muffins) | **Preparation Time:** 10 minutes | **Cooking Time:** 20 minutes

Ingredients:

- 6 large eggs
- 1/2 cup heavy cream
- 1/4 cup pesto (homemade or store-bought, sugar-free)
- 1/2 cup shredded mozzarella cheese
- 1/4 cup sun-dried tomatoes, chopped (oil-packed, drained)
- 1/4 cup fresh spinach, finely chopped
- Salt and pepper, to taste
- Butter or oil, for greasing muffin tins
- 1/4 cup cooked bacon bits or cooked crumbled sausage

Optional for garnish:
- Fresh basil leaves
- Extra pesto for drizzling
- Parmesan cheese, grated

Instructions:

1. Preheat the Oven: Set your oven to 350°F (175°C). Grease Muffin Tin: Use butter or oil to thoroughly grease a 12-cup muffin tin to prevent sticking.
2. Mix the Ingredients. In a large bowl, whisk together the eggs and heavy cream until well blended. Stir in the pesto, mozzarella cheese, sun-dried tomatoes, spinach, and optional bacon bits or sausage. Season with salt, pepper.
3. Fill Muffin Cups. Evenly distribute the egg mixture among the prepared muffin cups, filling each about 3/4 full to allow space for the muffins to rise.
4. Bake the Muffins: Place the muffin tin in the preheated oven and bake for 18-20 minutes, or until the tops are firm and just starting to turn golden.
5. Cool and Serve. Remove the muffin tin from the oven and let the muffins cool for a few minutes before removing them from the tin. Garnish with fresh basil, a drizzle of extra pesto, and a sprinkle of grated Parmesan cheese if desired.

Nutritional Information (Per Serving):

Calories: 220 kcal | Protein: 12 g | Carbohydrates: 3 g
Fats: 18 g | Cholesterol: 215 mg | Sodium: 300 mg
Potassium: 200 mg

Almond Butter and Blueberry Smoothie

 Yield:
1 servings   Preparation Time:
5 minutes   Cooking Time:
0 minutes

Ingredients:

- 1/4 cup blueberries (fresh or frozen)
- 2 tablespoons almond butter
- 1 cup unsweetened almond milk
- 1/4 cup heavy cream
- 1 tablespoon flaxseed meal
- 1 scoop vanilla protein powder (low-carb)
- Sweetener to taste (e.g., stevia, erythritol)
- A few whole blueberries
- A sprinkle of chia seeds

Instructions:

1. Prepare the Ingredients. Assemble all the ingredients. If using frozen blueberries, there's no need to thaw them as they help to chill the smoothie.
2. Combine Ingredients in Blender: Add the blueberries, almond butter, almond milk, heavy cream, flaxseed meal, protein powder to a blender. Blend on high until the mixture is smooth and creamy. Taste and add sweetener as needed.
3. Serve. Pour the smoothie into a serving glass. Garnish with a few whole blueberries, a sprinkle of chia seeds.

Keto Zucchini and Egg Breakfast Bowl

Yield:
2 servings   Preparation Time:
10 minutes Cooking Time:
10 minutes

Ingredients:

- 2 medium zucchini, spiralized or shredded
- 4 large eggs
- 4 slices of bacon, chopped
- 1/2 cup cherry tomatoes, halved
- 1/4 cup grated Parmesan cheese
- 2 tablespoons olive oil
- Salt and pepper, to taste
- 1/2 teaspoon garlic powder
- Avocado slices
- Sour cream

Instructions:

1. Cook the Bacon. In a large skillet, cook the chopped bacon over medium heat until crispy. Remove the bacon and set aside on a paper towel to drain.
2. Cook the Zucchini. In the same skillet, add 1 tablespoon of olive oil. Add the spiralized or shredded zucchini and sauté for 3-4 minutes until tender but still firm. Season with salt, pepper, and garlic powder.
3. Prepare the Eggs. In another skillet, heat the remaining tablespoon of olive oil. Crack the eggs into the skillet and scramble until fully cooked. Season with salt and pepper to taste.
4. Assemble the Bowls. Divide the cooked zucchini between two bowls. Top each with scrambled eggs and crispy bacon. Add cherry tomatoes and sprinkle with Parmesan cheese.
5. Garnish and Serve. Garnish with avocado slices and a dollop of sour cream. Enjoy your keto-friendly breakfast bowl warm!

Nutritional Information (Per Serving):

Calories: 450 kcal | Protein: 20 g | Carbohydrates: 12 g
Fats: 38 g | Cholesterol: 80 mg | Sodium: 200 mg
Potassium: 300 mg

Nutritional Information (Per Serving):

Calories: 450 kcal | Protein: 22 g | Carbohydrates: 10 g
Fats: 36 g | Cholesterol: 390 mg | Sodium: 750 mg
Potassium: 600 mg

Caramel Pecan Porridge

 Yield: 2 servings **Preparation Time:** 5 minutes **Cooking Time:** 10 minutes

Ingredients:

- 1 cup almond flour
- 1/4 cup ground flaxseed
- 2 tablespoons chia seeds
- 1 cup unsweetened almond milk
- 1/2 cup heavy cream
- 1/4 cup crushed pecans
- 2 tablespoons butter
- 2 tablespoons sugar-free caramel syrup
- 1/2 teaspoon vanilla extract
- Pinch of salt

Optional for garnish:
- Whipped cream (sugar-free)
- Additional crushed pecans
- Extra drizzle of sugar-free caramel syrup

Instructions:

1. Prepare the Porridge Base. In a medium saucepan, combine almond flour, ground flaxseed, and chia seeds. Mix thoroughly to distribute evenly. Pour in the almond milk and heavy cream, stirring constantly to ensure there are no lumps.
2. Cook the Porridge. Place the saucepan over medium heat. Bring the mixture to a gentle boil, stirring frequently to prevent sticking. Cook until the porridge begins to thicken, approximately 5-7 minutes. Stir in the butter, sugar-free caramel syrup, vanilla extract, and a pinch of salt. Mix well until the butter is melted and incorporated.
3. Add Pecans. Once the porridge has thickened to your liking, stir in the crushed pecans, reserving some for garnish if desired.
4. Serve. Divide the porridge into bowls. Top with a dollop of whipped cream, additional crushed pecans, and an extra drizzle of caramel syrup if desired.

Nutritional Information (Per Serving):

Calories: 550 kcal | Protein: 12 g | Carbohydrates: 14 g
Fats: 50 g | Cholesterol: 80 mg | Sodium: 200 mg
Potassium: 300 mg

Spinach and Mushroom Quiche

 Yield: 6 servings **Preparation Time:** 15 minutes **Cooking Time:** 35-40 minutes

Ingredients:

- Crust:
- 1 1/2 cups almond flour
- 1/4 cup coconut flour
- 1/4 cup unsalted butter, melted
- 1 large egg
- 1/2 tsp salt
- Filling:
- 1 tbsp olive oil or butter
- 1/2 cup onion, finely diced
- 2 cups mushrooms, sliced
- 2 cups fresh spinach
- 4 large eggs
- 1/2 cup heavy cream
- 1 cup shredded cheddar cheese
- Salt and pepper, to taste
- Optional Garnish:
- Fresh parsley or chives, chopped
- A sprinkle of grated Parmesan

Instructions:

1. Preheat your oven to 350°F (175°C). Grease a 9-inch pie dish with butter or olive oil.In a bowl, combine the almond flour, coconut flour, melted butter, egg, and salt. Mix until a dough forms. Press the dough evenly into the bottom and up the sides of the prepared pie dish. Bake the crust for 10 minutes until it is lightly golden. Remove from the oven and set aside.
2. Heat olive oil or butter in a large skillet over medium heat. Add the diced onions and cook for 3-4 minutes until softened. Add the mushrooms and cook for another 5-7 minutes until browned and tender. Add the spinach and cook for 1-2 minutes (or until wilted if using fresh spinach). Remove the skillet from heat.
3. In a mixing bowl, whisk together the eggs, heavy cream, shredded cheese, salt, pepper. Add the cooked mushroom and spinach mixture to the egg mixture, stirring until well combined. Pour the filling into the pre-baked crust, spreading it out evenly.
4. Place the quiche in the preheated oven and bake for 25-30 minutes, or until the filling is set and the top is golden brown. Remove from the oven and let the quiche cool for a few minutes before slicing.
5. Garnish with fresh parsley or chives and a sprinkle of grated Parmesan, if desired.

Nutritional Information (Per Serving):

Calories: 320 kcal | Protein: 12g | Carbohydrates: 6g
Fat: 28g | Cholesterol: 200mg | Sodium: 380mg
Potassium: 320mg

LUNCHES

Quick and satisfying midday meals

Keto Caesar Salad with Chicken

 Yield: 2 servings   **Preparation Time:** 20 minutes **Cooking Time:** 15 minutes

Ingredients:

For the Chicken:
- 2 chicken breasts (about 6 ounces each)
- 1 tablespoon olive oil
- Salt and pepper, to taste

For the Salad:
- 4 cups romaine lettuce, chopped
- 1/2 cup Parmesan cheese, shaved
- 1/4 cup low-carb Caesar dressing
- 2 tablespoons bacon bits
- 1/4 cup cherry tomatoes, halved

For the Homemade Caesar Dressing 1/2 cup mayonnaise
- 2 anchovy fillets, minced
- 1 garlic clove, minced
- 2 tablespoons lemon juice
- 1 teaspoon Worcestershire sauce (check for sugar-free)
- 1/2 teaspoon Dijon mustard
- 1/4 cup grated Parmesan cheese
- Salt and pepper, to taste

Instructions:

1. Prepare the Chicken. Season the chicken breasts with salt and pepper. Heat olive oil in a skillet over medium heat and cook the chicken for about 7 minutes on each side or until fully cooked and the internal temperature reaches 165°F (74°C). Remove from heat, let rest for a few minutes, and then slice thinly.
2. Make the Caesar Dressing. In a bowl, whisk together mayonnaise, anchovies, minced garlic, lemon juice, Worcestershire sauce, Dijon mustard, and grated Parmesan cheese. Season with salt and pepper to taste.
3. Assemble the Salad. In a large bowl, toss the chopped romaine lettuce with Caesar dressing until evenly coated. Add the shaved Parmesan cheese and bacon bits and toss again.
4. Serve. Divide the salad onto plates. Top with sliced chicken and optional cherry tomatoes. Sprinkle additional Parmesan cheese and crushed black pepper.

Nutritional Information (Per Serving):

Calories: 600 kcal | Protein: 40 g | Carbohydrates: 8 g
Fats: 46 g | Cholesterol: 125 mg | Sodium: 850 mg
Potassium: 650 mg

Avocado Shrimp Salad

 Yield: 2 servings   **Preparation Time:** 10 minutes **Cooking Time:** 5 minutes

Ingredients:

- 12 large shrimp, peeled and deveined
- 2 large avocados, diced
- 1/2 cup cherry tomatoes, halved
- 1/4 cup red onion, finely chopped
- 2 tablespoons cilantro, chopped
- 1 lime, juiced
- 2 tablespoons extra virgin olive oil
- 1 clove garlic, minced
- Salt and pepper, to taste

Instructions:

1. Cook the Shrimp. Heat a skillet over medium heat with 1 tablespoon olive oil. Add the shrimp, season with salt, pepper. Cook for 2-3 minutes per side or until pink and cooked through. Remove from heat and let cool slightly.
2. Prepare the Salad Base. In a large bowl, mix the diced avocados, cherry tomatoes, red onion, and chopped cilantro. In a small bowl, whisk together the lime juice, remaining olive oil, minced garlic Season with salt, pepper.
3. Combine and Serve. Pour the dressing over the avocado mixture and gently toss to coat. Add the cooked shrimp to the salad and toss lightly to combine. Divide the salad between two plates. Garnish with additional cilantro and lime wedges if desired.

Nutritional Information (Per Serving):

Calories: 480 kcal | Protein: 25 g | Carbohydrates: 14 g
Fats: 38 g | Cholesterol: 180 mg | Sodium: 300 mg
Potassium: 900 mg

Tuna Niçoise Salad

🍽 **Yield:** 2 servings ❄ **Preparation Time:** 15 minutes ⏲ **Cooking Time:** 10 minutes

Ingredients:

- 2 cans of tuna in olive oil (5 ounces each), drained
- 4 cups mixed salad greens
- 4 hard-boiled eggs, quartered
- 1/2 cup cherry tomatoes, halved
- 1/2 cup cooked green beans, trimmed
- 1/4 cup black olives, pitted
- 2 tablespoons capers
- 1/4 red onion, thinly sliced

For the dressing:
- 1/3 cup extra virgin olive oil
- 2 tablespoons red wine vinegar
- 1 teaspoon Dijon mustard
- 1 garlic clove, minced
- Salt and pepper, to taste

Instructions:

1. Prepare the Eggs and Green Beans. Place eggs in a saucepan, cover with water, bring to a boil, then cover and turn off the heat. Let sit for 12 minutes, then cool in ice water and peel. Bring a small pot of water to a boil, add green beans, and cook for 2-3 minutes until tender-crisp. Drain and plunge into ice water to stop the cooking process.
2. Make the Dressing. In a small bowl, whisk together the olive oil, red wine vinegar, Dijon mustard, minced garlic, salt, and pepper until emulsified.
3. Assemble the Salad. Arrange the mixed salad greens on two plates. Distribute the tuna, hard-boiled eggs, cherry tomatoes, green beans, black olives, capers, and red onion evenly between the plates.
4. Drizzle the dressing over the salad components. Enjoy this refreshing and satisfying meal.

Nutritional Information (Per Serving):

Calories: 650 kcal | Protein: 40 g | Carbohydrates: 10 g
Fats: 50 g | Cholesterol: 430 mg | Sodium: 700 mg
Potassium: 800 mg

Turkey Bacon Ranch Wrap

🍽 **Yield:** 2 servings ❄ **Preparation Time:** 10 minutes ⏲ **Cooking Time:** 5 minutes *(if cooking bacon from scratch)*

Ingredients:

- 4 slices of turkey breast (thinly sliced)
- 4 slices of cooked bacon
- 2 large low-carb tortillas (coconut or almond flour based)
- 1/2 cup mixed greens (lettuce, spinach, or arugula)
- 1/4 cup sliced cherry tomatoes
- 1/4 cup shredded cheddar cheese
- 2 tablespoons ranch dressing (sugar-free)
- 1/4 avocado, sliced

For homemade keto ranch dressing:
- 1/2 cup mayonnaise
- 1/4 cup sour cream
- 1 teaspoon dried chives
- 1 teaspoon dried parsley
- 1/2 teaspoon dried dill
- 1/2 teaspoon garlic powder
- 1/2 teaspoon onion powder
- Salt and pepper to taste
- 2 tablespoons of water to thin, if needed

Instructions:

1. Prepare the Ranch Dressing. Combine mayonnaise, sour cream, chives, parsley, dill, garlic powder, onion powder, salt, and pepper in a bowl. Whisk until smooth. Adjust consistency with water if necessary. Refrigerate until needed.
2. Assemble the Wrap. If desired, gently warm the tortillas in a dry skillet or microwave to make them more pliable. Lay out the tortillas and spread each with a tablespoon of ranch dressing. Add two slices of turkey to each tortilla, followed by two slices of bacon. Top with mixed greens, cherry tomatoes, shredded cheese, and avocado. Carefully roll the tortillas tightly to enclose the filling. If needed, secure with toothpicks.
3. Cut each wrap in half and serve immediately or wrap in parchment paper for a portable meal.

Nutritional Information (Per Serving):

Calories: 450 kcal | Protein: 25 g | Carbohydrates: 10 g
Fats: 35 g | Cholesterol: 90 mg | Sodium: 800 mg
Potassium: 300 mg

Sausage and Peppers Skillet

 Yield:
4 servings Preparation Time:
10 minutes  Cooking Time:
20 minutes

Ingredients:

- 4 large Italian sausages (choose sugar-free, keto-friendly sausages)
- 2 tablespoons olive oil
- 1 red bell pepper, sliced
- 1 green bell pepper, sliced
- 1 yellow bell pepper, sliced
- 1 onion, sliced
- 2 cloves garlic, minced
- 1/2 teaspoon salt
- 1/2 teaspoon black pepper
- 1 teaspoon smoked paprika
- 1/2 cup chicken broth (low sodium)
- 2 tablespoons fresh parsley, chopped

Instructions:

1. Prepare the Ingredients. Wash and slice the bell peppers and onion. Mince the garlic.
2. Brown the Sausages. In a large skillet, heat olive oil over medium-high heat. Add the sausages to the skillet and cook until browned on all sides, about 5-7 minutes. Remove sausages and set aside.
3. Cook the Vegetables. In the same skillet, add the onions and bell peppers. Sauté until they start to soften, about 5 minutes. Add the minced garlic, salt, pepper, smoked paprika. Cook for another 2 minutes.
4. Simmer with Sausages. Pour in the chicken broth to deglaze the pan, scraping up any browned bits from the bottom. Return the sausages to the skillet. Reduce heat to medium-low, cover, and let simmer for about 10 minutes, or until the sausages are cooked through and the vegetables are tender.
5. Sprinkle with fresh parsley before serving. Serve hot directly from the skillet.

Nutritional Information (Per Serving):

Calories: 450 kcal | Protein: 22 g | Carbohydrates: 10 g
Fats: 36 g | Cholesterol: 85 mg | Sodium: 900 mg
Potassium: 400 mg

Cauliflower Fried Rice

 Yield:
4 servings Preparation Time:
15 minutes Cooking Time:
10 minutes

Ingredients:

- 1 medium head of cauliflower, riced (about 4 cups)
- 2 tablespoons sesame oil
- 1/4 cup soy sauce (or tamari for gluten-free)
- 2 cloves garlic, minced
- 1/2 cup onion, diced
- 1/2 cup carrots, diced (optional, if within carb limits)
- 1/2 cup peas (optional, if within carb limits)
- 2 eggs, beaten
- 2 tablespoons green onions, chopped
- Salt and pepper, to taste

Instructions:

1. Prepare Cauliflower. Pulse the cauliflower florets in a food processor until they resemble rice grains. Alternatively, grate the florets using a box grater.
2. Cook the Vegetables. Heat sesame oil in a large skillet or wok over medium heat. Add the onions and garlic, sautéing until the onions are translucent. Add the diced carrots and peas, cooking until they are just tender (about 3-5 minutes).
3. Add Cauliflower and Seasonings. Increase heat to medium-high and stir in the riced cauliflower. Pour the soy sauce over the top and stir everything together, cooking for about 5 minutes until the cauliflower is tender. Adjust flavor with salt and pepper.
4. Add Eggs and Optional Protein. Push the cauliflower mixture to the side of the skillet. Pour the beaten eggs into the cleared space and scramble them until fully cooked. Once the eggs are cooked, mix them into the cauliflower rice.
5. Garnish and Serve. Stir in the chopped green onions and remove from heat. Garnish with additional green onions and sesame seeds if desired.

Nutritional Information (Per Serving):

Calories: 150 kcal | Protein: 6 g | Carbohydrates: 12 g
Fats: 9 g | Cholesterol: 95 mg | Sodium: 900 mg
Potassium: 450 mg

Beef Taco Salad

 Yield: 4 servings    **Preparation Time:** 10 minutes   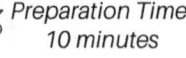 **Cooking Time:** 15 minutes

Ingredients:

- 1 pound ground beef (preferably 80/20)
- 1 tablespoon olive oil
- 2 teaspoons chili powder
- 1 teaspoon cumin
- 1/2 teaspoon garlic powder
- 1/2 teaspoon onion powder
- 1/4 teaspoon paprika
- Salt and pepper, to taste
- 8 cups mixed salad greens (such as romaine, iceberg, and spinach)
- 1 cup cherry tomatoes, halved
- 1/2 cup shredded cheddar cheese
- 1/4 cup red onion, finely chopped
- 1 avocado, diced
- 1/4 cup sour cream
- 1/4 cup salsa (sugar-free)
- 1/4 cup cilantro, chopped

Instructions:

1. Cook the Beef. Heat olive oil in a large skillet over medium heat. Add the ground beef, breaking it apart with a spoon. Cook until browned and no longer pink. Stir in chili powder, cumin, garlic powder, onion powder, paprika, salt, and pepper. Cook for an additional 2 minutes to blend the flavors. Remove from heat and set aside to cool slightly.
2. Prepare the Salad Base. In a large bowl, combine the mixed salad greens, cherry tomatoes, red onion, and shredded cheese.
3. Assemble the Salad. Add the cooked beef to the salad greens. Top with diced avocado, black olives.
4. Add Dressings and Garnishes. Dollop sour cream and salsa over the salad. Sprinkle chopped cilantro over the top.
5. Serve Immediately: Toss lightly before serving or let individuals dress their own portions as preferred.

Nutritional Information (Per Serving):

Calories: 500 kcal | Protein: 28 g | Carbohydrates: 10 g
Fats: 38 g | Cholesterol: 90 mg | Sodium: 400 mg
Potassium: 800 mg

Cobb Salad with Keto Vinaigrette

 Yield: 4 servings   **Preparation Time:** 15 minutes   **Cooking Time:** 10 minutes

Ingredients:

For the Salad:
- 4 cups mixed greens (such as romaine and arugula)
- 2 large eggs, hard-boiled and sliced
- 4 slices bacon, cooked and crumbled
- 1 medium avocado, diced
- 1/2 cup cherry tomatoes, halved
- 1/4 cup blue cheese, crumbled
- 1/2 cup cooked chicken breast, diced
- 1/4 red onion, thinly sliced

For the Keto Vinaigrette:
- 1/3 cup olive oil
- 2 tablespoons apple cider vinegar
- 1 teaspoon Dijon mustard
- 1 garlic clove, minced
- Salt and pepper to taste

Instructions:

1. Prepare the Ingredients. Place eggs in a saucepan, cover with water, and bring to a boil. Once boiling, cover and remove from heat. Let sit for 10 minutes, then cool in ice water and peel. Cook bacon in a skillet until crispy, drain, and crumble. Wash and dry mixed greens. Dice the avocado and chicken breast. Slice the red onion and halve the cherry tomatoes.
2. Make the Keto Vinaigrette. In a small bowl or jar, whisk together olive oil, apple cider vinegar, Dijon mustard, minced garlic, salt, and pepper until emulsified.
3. Assemble the Salad. In a large bowl or on individual plates, arrange the mixed greens. Neatly place rows of hard-boiled eggs, bacon, avocado, cherry tomatoes, blue cheese, chicken, and red onion over the greens.
4. Dress the Salad. Drizzle the keto vinaigrette over the salad just before serving to keep the ingredients fresh and crisp.
5. Garnish and Serve. Garnish with chopped fresh herbs if using. Enjoy this hearty and nutritious salad as a complete meal.

Nutritional Information (Per Serving):

Calories: 450 kcal | Protein: 25 g | Carbohydrates: 8 g
Fats: 36 g | Cholesterol: 185 mg | Sodium: 450 mg
Potassium: 600 mg

Spinach and Goat Cheese Stuffed Chicken

 Yield: 4 servings | **Preparation Time:** 15 minutes | **Cooking Time:** 25 minutes

Ingredients:

- 4 boneless, skinless chicken breasts
- 1 cup fresh spinach, chopped
- 4 ounces goat cheese
- 2 cloves garlic, minced
- 1/4 cup chopped walnuts (optional for added texture)
- 2 tablespoons olive oil
- Salt and pepper, to taste
- 1 teaspoon dried herbs (such as thyme or rosemary)

Instructions:

1. Prepare the Chicken. Preheat your oven to 375°F (190°C). Place each chicken breast between two sheets of plastic wrap and gently pound with a meat mallet or rolling pin to about 1/4 inch thickness.
2. Make the Stuffing. Heat 1 tablespoon of olive oil in a skillet over medium heat. Add the minced garlic and sauté for 30 seconds. Add the chopped spinach and cook until wilted, about 2-3 minutes. Remove from heat and let cool slightly. Mix in the goat cheese (and walnuts if using) until well combined.
3. Stuff and Secure. Lay out the flattened chicken breasts. Spread the spinach and goat cheese mixture evenly among the breasts. Roll up each breast tightly and secure with toothpicks.
4. Cook the Chicken. Season the outside of the chicken rolls with salt, pepper, and dried herbs. Heat the remaining olive oil in an oven-proof skillet over medium-high heat. Sear the chicken rolls until golden on all sides, about 3-4 minutes total. Transfer the skillet to the preheated oven and bake for 20 minutes, or until the chicken is cooked through and reaches an internal temperature of 165°F (74°C).
5. Serve. Let the chicken rest for a few minutes after baking. Remove toothpicks, slice if desired, and serve.

Nutritional Information (Per Serving):

Calories: 350 kcal | Protein: 28 g | Carbohydrates: 3 g
Fats: 25 g | Cholesterol: 80 mg | Sodium: 300 mg
Potassium: 400 mg

Pork Lettuce Wraps

 Yield: 4 servings | **Preparation Time:** 15 minutes | **Cooking Time:** 10 minutes

Ingredients:

- 1 pound ground pork
- 1 tablespoon sesame oil
- 2 cloves garlic, minced
- 1 inch fresh ginger, grated
- 1/4 cup soy sauce (or tamari for gluten-free option)
- 1 tablespoon rice vinegar
- 1 teaspoon chili paste
- 1/2 cup green onions, chopped
- 1/2 cup fresh cilantro, chopped
- 1/4 cup crushed peanuts (optional for added crunch)
- 8 large lettuce leaves (such as butter lettuce or iceberg)
- Salt and pepper, to taste

Instructions:

1. Cook the Pork. In a large skillet, heat the sesame oil over medium heat. Add the ground pork, breaking it apart with a spatula. Cook until the pork is browned and no longer pink, about 5-7 minutes. Stir in the minced garlic and grated ginger, cooking for another minute until fragrant.
2. Season the Pork. Pour the soy sauce, rice vinegar, and chili paste into the skillet. Stir well to combine all ingredients. Allow the mixture to simmer for a few minutes, letting the flavors meld together. Season with salt and pepper to taste.
3. Prepare the Lettuce and Garnishes. Wash and dry the lettuce leaves, ensuring they are whole and can hold the filling. Chop the green onions and cilantro. Crush the peanuts if using.
4. Assemble the Wraps. Spoon the cooked pork mixture into the center of each lettuce leaf. Top with green onions, cilantro, and crushed peanuts.
5. Serve Immediately: Enjoy the wraps fresh for the best texture and flavor.

Nutritional Information (Per Serving):

Calories: 350 kcal | Protein: 22 g | Carbohydrates: 6 g
Fats: 26 g | Cholesterol: 80 mg | Sodium: 800 mg
Potassium: 400 mg

Zucchini Noodle Caprese

 Yield:
2 servings   Preparation Time:
10 minutes   Cooking Time:
5 minutes

Ingredients:

- 2 large zucchinis
- 1 cup cherry tomatoes, halved
- 4 ounces fresh mozzarella cheese, cubed
- 1/4 cup fresh basil leaves, chopped
- 2 tablespoons olive oil
- 1 tablespoon balsamic vinegar (make sure it's low in sugars)
- Salt and pepper, to taste
- 1 garlic clove, minced (optional)

Optional for garnish:
- Extra basil leaves
- Drizzle of extra virgin olive oil
- Red pepper flakes, for a bit of spice

Instructions:

1. Prepare the Zucchini Noodles. Use a spiralizer to turn the zucchini into noodles. If you don't have a spiralizer, use a vegetable peeler to create thin ribbons. Heat a large skillet over medium heat. Add 1 tablespoon olive oil and the minced garlic (if using). Sauté the zucchini noodles for 2-3 minutes, just until tender. Season with salt and pepper. Remove from heat and allow to cool slightly in the pan.
2. Mix the Caprese Ingredients. In a large bowl, mix the halved cherry tomatoes, cubed mozzarella, and chopped basil with the zucchini noodles. Toss gently to combine.
3. Dress the Salad. Whisk together the remaining olive oil and balsamic vinegar. Season with salt and pepper to taste. Drizzle the dressing over the zucchini noodle mixture and toss to coat evenly.
4. Garnish and Serve: Divide the salad between plates. Garnish with extra basil leaves, a drizzle of extra virgin olive oil, and red pepper flakes if desired.

Nutritional Information (Per Serving):

Calories: 350 kcal | Protein: 15 g | Carbohydrates: 8 g
Fats: 28 g | Cholesterol: 45 mg | Sodium: 320 mg
Potassium: 500 mg

Cheesy Taco Skillet

 Yield:
4 servings   Preparation Time:
10 minutes   Cooking Time:
20 minutes

Ingredients:

- 1 pound ground beef (80/20 fat content)
- 1 medium onion, diced
- 1 bell pepper, diced
- 2 cloves garlic, minced
- 1 tablespoon taco seasoning
- 1 cup diced tomatoes (canned and drained)
- 1 cup shredded cheddar cheese
- 1/4 cup heavy cream
- 2 tablespoons olive oil
- Salt and pepper, to taste

Instructions:

1. Brown the Beef. Heat the olive oil in a large skillet over medium-high heat. Add the ground beef and season with salt and pepper. Cook until browned and crumbly, about 5-7 minutes.
2. Add Vegetables. Add the diced onion, bell pepper, and garlic to the skillet with the beef. Cook until the vegetables are softened, about 5 minutes.
3. Add Flavor. Stir in the taco seasoning and diced tomatoes. Reduce heat to medium and let simmer for about 5 minutes until the mixture thickens slightly.
4. Creamy Cheesy Mixture. Pour in the heavy cream and half of the shredded cheese into the skillet. Stir until the cheese melts and the mixture becomes creamy.
5. Add Cheese and Serve. Sprinkle the remaining cheese over the top. Cover the skillet with a lid and let the cheese melt, about 3 minutes.

Nutritional Information (Per Serving):

Calories: 500 kcal | Protein: 28 g | Carbohydrates: 9 g
Fats: 40 g | Cholesterol: 120 mg | Sodium: 500 mg
Potassium: 400 mg

Pulled Pork with Cabbage Slaw

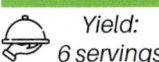 **Yield:** 6 servings **Preparation Time:** 20 minutes **Cooking Time:** 4 hours *(slow cooker on high)* or 8 hours *(on low)*

Ingredients:

For the Pulled Pork:
- 2 pounds pork shoulder
- 1 tablespoon paprika
- 1 teaspoon garlic powder
- 1 teaspoon onion powder
- 1 teaspoon salt
- 1/2 teaspoon black pepper
- 1/2 cup chicken broth
- 2 tablespoons apple cider vinegar
- 1 tablespoon Worcestershire sauce

For the Cabbage Slaw:
- 4 cups shredded cabbage
- 1/4 cup mayonnaise
- 1 tablespoon Dijon mustard
- 2 tablespoons apple cider vinegar
- 1 teaspoon erythritol
- Salt and pepper, to taste

Instructions:

1. Prepare the Pulled Pork. Mix paprika, garlic powder, onion powder, salt, and black pepper. Rub this mixture all over the pork shoulder. Place the seasoned pork in a slow cooker. Add chicken broth, apple cider vinegar, and Worcestershire sauce. Cover and cook on high for 4 hours or on low for 8 hours, until the pork is very tender and shreds easily. Remove the pork from the slow cooker and shred it using two forks. Optionally, mix some of the cooking juices back into the pork to keep it moist.
2. Make the Cabbage Slaw. In a large bowl, combine shredded cabbage, mayonnaise, Dijon mustard, apple cider vinegar, erythritol, salt, and pepper. Toss until well mixed. Refrigerate the slaw for at least 30 minutes before serving to allow flavors to meld.
3. Serve the pulled pork topped accompanied by a generous helping of cabbage slaw.

Nutritional Information (Per Serving):

Calories: 380 kcal | Protein: 25 g | Carbohydrates: 5 g
Fats: 28 g | Cholesterol: 90 mg | Sodium: 550 mg
Potassium: 500 mg

Keto Sushi Rolls

 Yield: 4 servings *(2 rolls per serving)* **Preparation Time:** 20 minutes **Cooking Time:** 0 minutes

Ingredients:

- 8 nori sheets
- 2 cups cauliflower rice (see instructions below)
- 1 tablespoon rice vinegar (sugar-free)
- 1/2 teaspoon salt
- 1/4 teaspoon sugar substitute (e.g., erythritol)
- 8 ounces cream cheese, softened
- 1 cucumber, julienned
- 1 avocado, thinly sliced
- 8 ounces smoked salmon or cooked shrimp
- Soy sauce or tamari (gluten-free), for serving
- Wasabi and pickled ginger, for serving

Instructions:

1. Prepare the Cauliflower Rice. Pulse cauliflower florets in a food processor until they resemble rice grains. Heat a skillet over medium heat, add the cauliflower rice, and dry sauté for about 5-7 minutes until tender. Allow to cool slightly. Mix in rice vinegar, salt, and sugar substitute. Set aside to cool completely.
2. Assemble the Sushi Rolls. Place a nori sheet shiny-side down on a bamboo sushi mat. Spread about 1/4 cup of the cauliflower rice evenly over the nori, leaving about an inch clear at the top of the sheet to seal the roll. Layer strips of cucumber, avocado slices, and smoked salmon or shrimp along the bottom edge of the rice-covered nori. Lift the edge of the bamboo mat over the filling, tucking the nori to start a roll. Use the mat to compress the roll as you continue to roll the sushi away from you, peeling back the mat as you go. Moisten the exposed strip of nori at the top with a little water to help seal the sushi roll.
3. Cut and Serve. Use a sharp knife to slice each roll into six pieces. Wipe the knife with a wet cloth between slices to make a clean cut. Arrange sushi rolls on a plate. Serve with soy sauce or tamari, wasabi, and pickled ginger.

Nutritional Information (Per Serving):

Calories: 300 kcal | Protein: 15 g | Carbohydrates: 10 g
Fats: 22 g | Cholesterol: 50 mg | Sodium: 700 mg
Potassium: 400 mg

Creamy Tomato Basil Soup

 Yield: 4 servings   **Preparation Time:** 10 minutes   **Cooking Time:** 30 minutes

Ingredients:

- 2 tablespoons olive oil
- 1 medium onion, diced
- 2 cloves garlic, minced
- 1 (28-ounce) can crushed tomatoes
- 1 cup chicken or vegetable broth
- 1 cup heavy cream
- 1/4 cup fresh basil leaves, chopped
- Salt and pepper, to taste
- 1/2 teaspoon dried oregano
- Red pepper flakes, to taste
- Grated Parmesan cheese, for garnish
- Additional fresh basil, for garnish

Instructions:

1. Sauté the Base Ingredients. In a large pot, heat the olive oil over medium heat. Add the diced onion and sauté until translucent, about 5 minutes. Add the minced garlic and cook for an additional 1 minute until fragrant.
2. Add Tomatoes and Simmer. Stir in the crushed tomatoes and dried oregano. Cook for a few minutes to let the flavors combine. Pour in the broth and bring the mixture to a simmer. Reduce heat and let simmer for 20 minutes, stirring occasionally.
3. Blend the Soup. Using an immersion blender, blend the soup directly in the pot until smooth. If you don't have an immersion blender, carefully transfer the soup to a blender in batches and blend until smooth.
4. Add Cream and Season. Return the blended soup to the pot if needed and stir in the heavy cream and chopped fresh basil. Warm through. Season with salt and pepper to taste. Add red pepper flakes if using for a little heat.
5. Garnish and Serve: Ladle the soup into bowls. Garnish with grated Parmesan cheese and additional basil leaves if desired.

Nutritional Information (Per Serving):

Calories: 290 kcal | Protein: 5 g | Carbohydrates: 14 g
Fats: 25 g | Cholesterol: 80 mg | Sodium: 300 mg
Potassium: 500 mg

Creamy Chicken and Asparagus

 Yield: 4 servings   **Preparation Time:** 15 minutes   **Cooking Time:** 25 minutes

Ingredients:

- 4 boneless, skinless chicken breasts
- 1 tablespoon olive oil
- 1 tablespoon butter
- 1 pound asparagus, trimmed and cut into thirds
- 1 cup heavy cream
- 1/2 cup chicken broth
- 1 teaspoon garlic powder
- 1 teaspoon onion powder
- 1/2 cup grated Parmesan cheese
- Salt and pepper, to taste
- 1/4 cup fresh parsley, chopped (for garnish)

Instructions:

1. Cook the Chicken. Season the chicken breasts with salt, pepper, garlic powder, and onion powder. Heat olive oil and butter in a large skillet over medium-high heat. Add chicken breasts and cook for about 5-7 minutes on each side, or until golden brown and nearly cooked through. Remove from skillet and set aside.
2. Cook the Asparagus. In the same skillet, add the asparagus and sauté for 3-4 minutes, or until just tender but still crisp. Remove from skillet and set aside.
3. Make the Cream Sauce. Pour chicken broth into the skillet to deglaze, scraping up any browned bits. Stir in heavy cream and bring to a simmer. Reduce heat and add Parmesan cheese, stirring until melted and smooth. If using, add lemon zest, lemon juice, and red pepper flakes now. Return the chicken and asparagus to the skillet. Spoon the sauce over the chicken and asparagus, cooking for an additional 3-5 minutes until the chicken is fully cooked.
4. Garnish and Serve. Sprinkle with fresh parsley before serving. Dish can be served with a side of keto-friendly cauliflower rice or enjoyed on its own.

Nutritional Information (Per Serving):

Calories: 450 kcal | Protein: 29 g | Carbohydrates: 6 g
Fats: 35 g | Cholesterol: 145 mg | Sodium: 320 mg
Potassium: 500 mg

Keto Lasagna

🍽 Yield: 6 servings ⚙ Preparation Time: 20 minutes ⏲ Cooking Time: 40 minutes

Ingredients:

- For the "Noodles":
- 3 large eggs
- 4 oz cream cheese, softened
- 1/3 cup Parmesan cheese, grated
- 1/4 teaspoon ground black pepper
- 1 tablespoon Italian seasoning

- For the Filling:
- 1 pound ground beef
- 1/2 cup onion, chopped
- 2 cloves garlic, minced
- 1 cup marinara sauce (sugar-free)
- 1 cup ricotta cheese
- 1 cup mozzarella cheese, shredded

Instructions:

1. Prepare the Keto Noodles. Preheat your oven to 375°F (190°C). In a blender, combine eggs, cream cheese, Parmesan cheese, black pepper, and Italian seasoning. Blend until smooth. Pour the mixture into a lined baking sheet or silicone baking mat. Spread evenly to form a rectangle. Bake for 15-20 minutes, until set. Once cooked, set aside to cool, then cut into lasagna noodle-sized strips.
2. Prepare the Meat Sauce. In a skillet, brown the ground beef over medium heat. Add onions and garlic and cook until onions are translucent. Stir in the marinara sauce and optional red pepper flakes. Simmer for 10 minutes. Season with salt and pepper to taste.
3. Assemble the Lasagna. In a baking dish, lay down a layer of the prepared noodles. Top with a layer of the meat sauce, followed by dollops of ricotta, and sprinkle a layer of mozzarella. Repeat the layering process until all ingredients are used up, finishing with a cheese layer on top. Bake in the preheated oven for 20 minutes or until the cheese is bubbly and golden.
4. Serve. Let the lasagna sit for 5-10 minutes before slicing. This helps the layers set and makes it easier to serve.

Nutritional Information (Per Serving):

Calories: 450 kcal | Protein: 32 g | Carbohydrates: 6 g
Fats: 34 g | Cholesterol: 180 mg | Sodium: 500 mg
Potassium: 400 mg

Cream of Mushroom Soup

🍽 Yield: 4 servings ⚙ Preparation Time: 10 minutes ⏲ Cooking Time: 25 minutes

Ingredients:

- 1 pound fresh mushrooms, finely chopped (button or cremini work well)
- 3 tablespoons unsalted butter
- 1 small onion, finely chopped
- 2 cloves garlic, minced
- 1 teaspoon dried thyme
- 1/2 teaspoon salt
- 1/4 teaspoon black pepper
- 3 cups chicken or vegetable broth (low sodium)
- 1 cup heavy cream
- 2 tablespoons almond flour (to thicken, optional)
- 2 tablespoons fresh parsley, chopped (for garnish)

Instructions:

1. Sauté Vegetables. In a large pot, melt the butter over medium heat. Add the chopped mushrooms and onion to the pot. Cook until the mushrooms have released their moisture and the onions are translucent, about 7-10 minutes. Stir in the minced garlic, thyme, salt, and pepper. Cook for an additional 1-2 minutes until fragrant.
2. Deglaze and Simmer. If using, pour in the white wine and allow it to reduce slightly, about 2-3 minutes. Pour in the chicken or vegetable broth. Bring to a simmer and cook for 10 minutes, letting the flavors meld together.
3. Thicken the Soup. If a thicker soup is desired, whisk almond flour into the soup to thicken it, ensuring there are no clumps. Reduce the heat to low and stir in the heavy cream. Warm through but do not boil, to prevent curdling.
4. Garnish and Serve: Ladle the soup into bowls. Garnish with freshly chopped parsley and a sprinkle of nutmeg if using.

Nutritional Information (Per Serving):

Calories: 300 kcal | Protein: 6 g | Carbohydrates: 8 g
Fats: 28 g | Cholesterol: 85 mg | Sodium: 300 mg
Potassium: 300 mg

Keto Reuben Sandwich

 Yield: 4 servings | Preparation Time: 10 minutes | Cooking Time: 10 minutes

Keto Baked Pumpkin Slices with Herbs and Garlic

 Yield: 4 servings | Preparation Time: 10 minutes | Cooking Time: 30 minutes

Ingredients:

For the Sandwich:
- 8 slices of keto bread
- 8 ounces corned beef, thinly sliced
- 8 slices Swiss cheese
- 1 cup sauerkraut, drained
- Butter, for grilling the sandwich

For the Keto Dressing:
- 1/2 cup mayonnaise
- 2 tablespoons sugar-free ketchup
- 1 tablespoon finely chopped dill pickle
- 1 teaspoon Worcestershire sauce
- 1 teaspoon hot sauce (optional, adjust to taste)
- Salt and pepper, to taste

Instructions:

1. Prepare the Keto Dressing. In a small bowl, combine mayonnaise, sugar-free ketchup, chopped dill pickle, Worcestershire sauce, and hot sauce. Stir until well blended. Season with salt and pepper to taste. Set aside.
2. Assemble the Sandwiches. Spread a generous amount of the keto Russian dressing on one side of each slice of keto bread. On four slices of bread, layer the corned beef, Swiss cheese, and sauerkraut. Place the other slices of bread on top, dressing side down, to complete each sandwich.
3. Grill the Sandwiches. Heat a skillet over medium heat. Butter the outside of each sandwich and place in the skillet. Grill for about 3-5 minutes on each side, or until the bread is golden brown and the cheese has melted.
4. Cut the sandwiches in half, if desired, and serve hot.

Ingredients:

- 1 small pumpkin (about 2-3 lbs, peeled, seeded, and cut into thin slices)
- 4 tbsp olive oil
- 3 cloves garlic, minced
- 1 tsp dried thyme
- 1 tsp dried rosemary
- Salt and pepper, to taste
- 2 tbsp fresh parsley, chopped (optional, for garnish)
- 1 tbsp lemon zest (optional, for added freshness)

Instructions:

1. Preheat your oven to 400°F (200°C). Line a baking sheet with parchment paper or a silicone baking mat. Peel and seed the pumpkin, then cut it into thin slices, about 1/4-inch thick.
2. In a large mixing bowl, combine the olive oil, minced garlic, thyme, rosemary, smoked paprika (if using), salt, and pepper. Toss the pumpkin slices in the herb and oil mixture until they are evenly coated.
3. Lay the seasoned pumpkin slices in a single layer on the prepared baking sheet. Make sure they are not overlapping for even cooking. Bake in the preheated oven for 25-30 minutes, flipping the slices halfway through, until they are golden brown and tender.
4. Once the pumpkin slices are baked, remove them from the oven. Optionally, sprinkle with fresh parsley and lemon zest for an added burst of flavor. Serve warm as a side dish or light keto snack.

Nutritional Information (Per Serving):

Calories: 450 kcal | Protein: 25 g | Carbohydrates: 8 g
Fats: 36 g | Cholesterol: 95 mg | Sodium: 1200 mg
Potassium: 200 m

Nutritional Information (Per Serving):

Calories: 170 kcal | Protein: 2g | Carbohydrates: 8g
Fat: 14g | Cholesterol: 0mg | Sodium: 250mg
Potassium: 410mg

DINNERS

Delicious dishes to enjoy in the evenings.

Keto Cheesy Cauliflower Bake

Yield: 6 servings | Preparation Time: 15 minutes | Cooking Time: 25 minutes

Keto Chicken Parmesan

Yield: 4 servings | Preparation Time: 15 minutes | Cooking Time: 30 minutes

Ingredients:

- 1 large head cauliflower, cut into florets
- 3 tablespoons unsalted butter
- 1 cup heavy cream
- 1 teaspoon garlic powder
- 1/2 teaspoon onion powder
- 1/2 teaspoon salt
- 1/4 teaspoon black pepper
- 1/4 teaspoon paprika
- 1 and 1/2 cups shredded cheddar cheese
- 1/2 cup grated Parmesan cheese

Optional for added flavor:

- 2 tablespoons fresh chives, chopped
- 1/4 cup bacon bits

Instructions:

1. Preheat your oven to 375°F (190°C). Bring a large pot of water to a boil. Add cauliflower florets and cook for 5-7 minutes until just tender. Drain well and set aside.
2. Make Cheese Sauce. In a saucepan, melt butter over medium heat. Stir in heavy cream, garlic powder, onion powder, salt, black pepper, and paprika. Bring to a simmer. Reduce heat and add 1 cup of cheddar cheese and all the Parmesan cheese. Stir until the cheeses are melted and the sauce is smooth.
3. Combine Ingredients. In a large mixing bowl, combine the drained cauliflower with the cheese sauce, ensuring all florets are well-coated.
4. Bake. Pour the cauliflower mixture into a greased baking dish. Sprinkle the remaining 1/2 cup of cheddar cheese over the top. Place in the oven and bake for 20-25 minutes, or until the top is golden and bubbly.
5. Garnish and Serve. Sprinkle chopped chives and bacon bits over the top before serving. Serve hot as a side dish or a main course.

Nutritional Information (Per Serving):

Calories: 350 kcal | Protein: 12 g | Carbohydrates: 8 g
Fats: 30 g | Cholesterol: 95 mg | Sodium: 450 mg
Potassium: 400 mg

Ingredients:

- 4 boneless, skinless chicken breasts
- 1 cup almond flour
- 1/2 cup grated Parmesan cheese
- 1 teaspoon garlic powder
- 1 teaspoon Italian seasoning
- Salt and pepper, to taste
- 2 large eggs
- 1/4 cup olive oil for frying
- 1 cup sugar-free marinara sauce
- 1 cup shredded mozzarella cheese

Instructions:

1. Prepare the Chicken. Place chicken breasts between two sheets of plastic wrap and pound with a meat mallet to even thickness about 1/2 inch. Season each breast with salt and pepper.
2. Breading Station. In a shallow dish, mix almond flour, grated Parmesan, garlic powder, and Italian seasoning. In another shallow dish, beat the eggs. Dip each chicken breast first in the egg wash, then in the almond flour mixture, ensuring a good coat.
3. Fry the Chicken. In a large skillet, heat olive oil over medium heat. Add the chicken and fry until golden brown on each side, about 4-5 minutes per side.
4. Bake. Preheat oven to 375°F (190°C). In a baking dish, spread half of the marinara sauce. Place fried chicken over the sauce, top with remaining marinara sauce, and sprinkle shredded mozzarella cheese evenly over the top. Place in the oven and bake for 20 minutes, or until the cheese is bubbly and slightly golden.
5. Serve: Serve hot with a side of keto-friendly vegetables, such as zucchini noodles or a green salad.

Nutritional Information (Per Serving):

Calories: 550 kcal | Protein: 40 g | Carbohydrates: 8 g
Fats: 40 g | Cholesterol: 180 mg | Sodium: 650 mg
Potassium: 300 mg

Low-Carb Beef Stroganoff

 Yield:
4 servings   **Preparation Time:**
10 minutes   **Cooking Time:**
20 minutes

Ingredients:
- 1 pound beef sirloin or tenderloin, thinly sliced
- 2 tablespoons olive oil
- 1 medium onion, thinly sliced
- 2 cloves garlic, minced
- 8 ounces mushrooms, sliced
- 1 teaspoon paprika
- 1/2 cup beef broth (preferably low sodium)
- 1 cup sour cream
- Salt and pepper, to taste
- 2 tablespoons fresh parsley, chopped (for garnish)

Instructions:
1. Brown the Beef. Heat olive oil over medium-high heat. Season the beef slices with salt and pepper and add them to the skillet. Cook until browned on all sides, about 3-4 minutes. Remove the beef from the skillet and set aside.
2. Sauté Vegetables. In the same skillet, add the onions and mushrooms. Sauté until the onions are translucent and the mushrooms have released their moisture, about 5-7 minutes. Stir in the minced garlic and paprika, cooking for another minute until fragrant.
3. Deglaze and Simmer. If using white wine, pour it in now and let it reduce slightly. Then add the beef broth and bring to a simmer. Let the mixture simmer gently for about 10 minutes or until slightly reduced.
4. Add Beef and Sour Cream. Return the browned beef to the skillet. Lower the heat and stir in the sour cream. Heat through but do not boil, to prevent the sauce from curdling.
5. Garnish and Serve. Adjust salt and pepper to taste. Sprinkle with chopped fresh parsley before serving.

Nutritional Information (Per Serving):
Calories: 400 kcal | Protein: 25 g | Carbohydrates: 8 g
Fats: 30 g | Cholesterol: 90 mg | Sodium: 300 mg
Potassium: 650 mg

Thai Coconut Curry Shrimp

 Yield:
4 servings   **Preparation Time:**
15 minutes   **Cooking Time:**
20 minutes

Ingredients:
- 1 pound shrimp, peeled and deveined
- 2 tablespoons coconut oil
- 1 medium onion, finely chopped
- 2 cloves garlic, minced
- 1 tablespoon fresh ginger, minced
- 1 red bell pepper, sliced
- 1 green bell pepper, sliced
- 3 tablespoons red curry paste
- 1 can (14 ounces) full-fat coconut milk
- 1 tablespoon fish sauce
- 1 tablespoon erythritol
- Juice of 1 lime
- Salt to taste
- 1/4 cup fresh cilantro, chopped (for garnish)
- 1/4 cup fresh basil leaves, chopped (for garnish)

Instructions:
1. Prepare the Ingredients. Ensure shrimp are thawed, peeled, and deveined. Prepare onion, garlic, ginger, and bell peppers as noted.
2. Sauté Vegetables. In a large skillet or wok, heat coconut oil over medium heat. Add onion, garlic, and ginger to the skillet. Sauté for 2-3 minutes until onions are translucent. Incorporate red and green bell peppers and cook for an additional 3-4 minutes.
3. Make the Curry. Stir in red curry paste and cook for 1 minute until fragrant. Add the full can of coconut milk, fish sauce, erythritol, and optional lemongrass. Bring to a gentle simmer, stirring continuously.
4. Cook the Shrimp. Place the shrimp in the curry and cook for 5-6 minutes or until they are pink and fully cooked. Squeeze in lime juice and add salt to taste. Adjust seasoning with chili flakes if desired.
5. Garnish and Serve. Sprinkle chopped cilantro and basil over the curry before serving. Serve hot, accompanied by keto-friendly cauliflower rice or steamed vegetables.

Nutritional Information (Per Serving):
Calories: 350 kcal | Protein: 25 g | Carbohydrates: 9 g
Fats: 25 g | Cholesterol: 185 mg | Sodium: 800 mg
Potassium: 300 mg

Zucchini Lasagna

 Yield: 6 servings   **Preparation Time:** 20 minutes   **Cooking Time:** 45 minutes

Ingredients:

- 3 large zucchinis, sliced lengthwise into thin strips
- 1 tablespoon olive oil
- 1 pound ground beef
- 1 small onion, chopped
- 2 cloves garlic, minced
- 1 cup sugar-free marinara sauce
- 1 cup ricotta cheese
- 1 cup mozzarella cheese, shredded
- 1/2 cup Parmesan cheese, grated
- 1 egg
- 1 tablespoon Italian seasoning

Instructions:

1. Prepare the Zucchini. Cut zucchini into thin slices using a mandoline slicer or a sharp knife. Sprinkle salt on the slices and set them aside to release moisture. After 10 minutes, pat dry with paper towels to remove excess moisture.
2. Brown the Meat. Heat olive oil in a skillet over medium heat. Add chopped onion and garlic, sautéing until translucent. Add ground beef, breaking it up with a spoon, and cook until browned. Drain excess fat. Stir in the marinara sauce, red pepper flakes (if using), and Italian seasoning. Simmer for 10 minutes to let flavors meld. Season with salt and pepper.
3. Prepare Cheese Mixture. In a bowl, combine ricotta cheese, Parmesan cheese, and egg. Mix well until combined.
4. Assemble the Lasagna. In a baking dish, start with a layer of zucchini slices to cover the bottom. Spread half of the meat sauce over the zucchini, then half of the ricotta mixture, and sprinkle with a third of the mozzarella cheese. Repeat the layers, finishing with a top layer of zucchini and the remaining mozzarella. Preheat your oven to 375°F (190°C).
5. Bake. Cover the lasagna with foil and bake in the preheated oven for 30 minutes. Remove foil and bake for an additional 15 minutes, or until the cheese is golden and bubbly.
6. Serve. Let the lasagna cool for 10 minutes before serving.

Nutritional Information (Per Serving):

Calories: 350 kcal | Protein: 26 g | Carbohydrates: 8 g
Fats: 24 g | Cholesterol: 85 mg | Sodium: 500 mg
Potassium: 450 mg

Keto Meatloaf

 Yield: 6 servings   **Preparation Time:** 15 minutes   **Cooking Time:** 1 hour

Ingredients:

- 2 pounds ground beef (preferably 80/20 mix)
- 1/2 cup almond flour
- 1/4 cup heavy cream
- 2 large eggs
- 1/2 onion, finely chopped
- 2 cloves garlic, minced
- 1 tablespoon Worcestershire sauce
- 1 teaspoon salt
- 1/2 teaspoon black pepper
- 1/2 teaspoon smoked paprika
- 1/4 cup fresh parsley, chopped

For the topping:
- 1/3 cup sugar-free ketchup
- 2 tablespoons mustard
- 1 tablespoon erythritol

Instructions:

1. Preheat Oven and Prepare Baking Dish. Heat your oven to 350°F (175°C). Line a loaf pan with parchment paper or lightly grease it.
2. Mix the Meatloaf Ingredients. In a large bowl, mix the ground beef, almond flour, heavy cream, eggs, onion, garlic, Worcestershire sauce, salt, pepper, smoked paprika, and parsley. Mix well to combine. Transfer the meat mixture to the prepared loaf pan, pressing it into an even layer.
3. Prepare the Topping. In a small bowl, combine sugar-free ketchup, mustard, and erythritol. Spread the topping evenly over the meatloaf.
4. Bake. Place in the oven and bake for about 1 hour or until the meatloaf reaches an internal temperature of 160°F (71°C). Let the meatloaf rest for 10 minutes before slicing. This helps the juices redistribute.

Nutritional Information (Per Serving):

Calories: 450 kcal | Protein: 28 g | Carbohydrates: 5 g
Fats: 35 g | Cholesterol: 140 mg | Sodium: 600 mg
Potassium: 350 mg

Creamy Tuscan Garlic Chicken

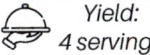 **Yield:** 4 servings   **Preparation Time:** 10 minutes   **Cooking Time:** 20 minutes

Ingredients:

- 4 boneless, skinless chicken breasts
- Salt and pepper, to taste
- 2 tablespoons olive oil
- 1 cup heavy cream
- 1/2 cup chicken broth
- 1 teaspoon garlic powder
- 1 teaspoon Italian seasoning
- 1/2 cup sun-dried tomatoes, chopped
- 1 cup spinach, fresh
- 1/2 cup grated Parmesan cheese

Instructions:

1. Prepare the Chicken. Season chicken breasts with salt, pepper, and garlic powder. Heat olive oil in a large skillet over medium heat. Add chicken breasts and cook until golden on each side and cooked through, about 6-8 minutes per side. Remove chicken and set aside.
2. Make the Sauce. In the same skillet, add minced garlic (if using) and sauté for about 1 minute until fragrant. Pour in chicken broth to deglaze the pan, scraping up any browned bits. Stir in heavy cream, Italian seasoning, and sun-dried tomatoes. Bring to a simmer. Add spinach and cook until wilted. Stir in Parmesan cheese until melted and the sauce is creamy.
3. Combine Chicken and Sauce. Return chicken to the skillet, spooning the sauce over the chicken. Cook for an additional 2-3 minutes to reheat the chicken and mingle the flavors.
4. Serve: Serve the chicken hot, drizzled with plenty of the creamy Tuscan sauce.

Nutritional Information (Per Serving):

Calories: 495 kcal | Protein: 29 g | Carbohydrates: 8 g
Fats: 40 g | Cholesterol: 145 mg | Sodium: 450 mg
Potassium: 550 mg

Seared Salmon with Creamy Dill Sauce

 Yield: 4 servings 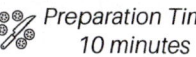 **Preparation Time:** 10 minutes   **Cooking Time:** 15 minutes

Ingredients:

- 4 salmon fillets (6 ounces each)
- 2 tablespoons olive oil
- Salt and pepper, to taste

For the Creamy Dill Sauce:
- 1 cup heavy cream
- 2 tablespoons unsalted butter
- 1 teaspoon garlic, minced
- 2 tablespoons fresh dill, chopped
- Juice of half a lemon
- Salt and pepper, to taste

Instructions:

1. Prepare the Salmon. Pat the salmon fillets dry with paper towels. Season both sides with salt and pepper. In a large skillet, heat olive oil over medium-high heat.
2. Sear the Salmon. Place salmon fillets skin-side down in the skillet. Cook for 5-6 minutes on each side, or until the skin is crispy and the salmon is cooked to your liking.
3. Make the Creamy Dill Sauce. In a saucepan, melt butter over medium heat. Add garlic and sauté for about 1 minute until fragrant. Pour in the heavy cream, add chopped dill, lemon juice, and optional capers and red pepper flakes. Reduce heat to low and simmer the sauce for about 3-4 minutes, stirring occasionally, until thickened. Taste and adjust seasoning with salt and pepper.
4. Serve. Place each salmon fillet on a plate. Spoon the creamy dill sauce over the salmon fillets.

Nutritional Information (Per Serving):

Calories: 495 kcal | Protein: 34 g | Carbohydrates: 3 g
Fats: 38 g | Cholesterol: 125 mg | Sodium: 300 mg
Potassium: 850 mg

Keto Shepherd's Pie

 Yield:
6 servings

 Preparation Time:
20 minutes

Cooking Time:
30 minutes

Ingredients:

- 1 pound ground beef or lamb
- 1 tablespoon olive oil
- 1 medium onion, chopped
- 2 cloves garlic, minced
- 1/2 cup chopped celery
- 1/2 cup chopped carrots
- 1 teaspoon salt
- 1/2 teaspoon black pepper
- 2 tablespoons tomato paste
- 1 cup beef broth
- 1 teaspoon Worcestershire sauce (ensure it's sugar-free)
- 1 teaspoon dried rosemary
- 1 teaspoon dried thyme
- For the topping:
- 1 large cauliflower, cut into florets
- 1/4 cup heavy cream
- 2 tablespoons unsalted butter
- 1/2 cup shredded cheddar cheese
- Salt and pepper, to taste

Instructions:

1. Prepare the Meat Filling. Heat olive oil in a large skillet over medium heat. Add onion and garlic and sauté until translucent. Add ground beef or lamb, salt, and pepper. Cook until browned. Stir in celery and carrots. Add tomato paste, beef broth, Worcestershire sauce, rosemary, and thyme. Simmer for about 10 minutes until the liquid reduces slightly and the flavors meld.
2. Make the Cauliflower Mash. Steam the cauliflower florets until very tender, about 10-15 minutes. Transfer to a food processor, add heavy cream, butter, and season with salt and pepper. Blend until smooth. Stir in cheddar cheese until well combined.
3. Assemble the Pie. In a baking dish, spread the meat mixture in an even layer. Top with the cauliflower mash, spreading evenly.
4. Preheat oven to 400°F (200°C). Bake the shepherd's pie for 20 minutes or until the top is golden and bubbly. Let sit for 5 minutes after baking.

Nutritional Information (Per Serving):

Calories: 400 kcal | Protein: 25 g | Carbohydrates: 8 g
Fats: 30 g | Cholesterol: 90 mg | Sodium: 600 mg
Potassium: 550 mg

Lemon Garlic Butter Steak

 Yield:
4 servings

 Preparation Time:
10 minutes

Cooking Time:
15 minutes

Ingredients:

- 4 ribeye or New York strip steaks (about 8 ounces each)
- Salt and freshly ground black pepper, to taste
- 2 tablespoons olive oil
- 4 tablespoons unsalted butter
- 3 cloves garlic, minced
- Juice of 1 lemon
- 1 teaspoon lemon zest
- 2 tablespoons fresh parsley, chopped

Instructions:

1. Prepare the Steaks. Pat the steaks dry with paper towels. Season generously with salt and pepper on both sides. Heat olive oil in a large skillet over high heat until very hot.
2. Cook the Steaks. Add the steaks to the hot skillet. Cook for about 3-4 minutes on each side for medium-rare or adjust the cooking time based on your preferred doneness. Remove steaks from the skillet and let them rest on a plate, loosely covered with foil.
3. Make the Garlic Lemon Butter Sauce. Reduce heat to medium and add butter to the same skillet. Once the butter has melted, add the minced garlic and optional herbs. Sauté for about 1-2 minutes until fragrant but not browned. Stir in lemon juice and zest. Cook for an additional minute to blend the flavors together.
4. Serve. Spoon the lemon garlic butter sauce over the rested steaks.

Nutritional Information (Per Serving):

Calories: 560 kcal | Protein: 48 g | Carbohydrates: 2 g
Fats: 42 g | Fiber: 0 g | Cholesterol: 135 mg | Sodium: 120 mg | Potassium: 600 mg

Spaghetti Squash Carbonara

 **Yield:** 4 servings | **Preparation Time:** 15 minutes | **Cooking Time:** 45 minutes

Ingredients:

- 1 large spaghetti squash (about 3 pounds)
- 2 tablespoons olive oil
- Salt and pepper, to taste
- 4 ounces pancetta or thick-cut bacon, diced
- 2 cloves garlic, minced
- 1/2 cup heavy cream
- 2 large eggs
- 1 cup grated Parmesan cheese
- 1/4 cup fresh parsley, chopped
- Freshly ground black pepper, to taste

Instructions:

1. Prepare the Spaghetti Squash. Preheat your oven to 400°F (200°C). Slice the spaghetti squash in half lengthwise and scoop out the seeds. Drizzle the inside of each half with olive oil and season with salt and pepper. Place cut side down on a baking sheet and roast in the oven for 30-40 minutes, or until the flesh easily shreds with a fork.
2. Cook the Pancetta. While the squash is baking, heat a large skillet over medium heat. Add the diced pancetta or bacon and cook until crisp. Remove pancetta from the skillet and set aside, leaving the fat in the pan.
3. Make the Carbonara Sauce. In a bowl, whisk together the heavy cream, eggs, and grated Parmesan cheese. In the same skillet used for pancetta, add minced garlic to the remaining fat and sauté for about 1 minute until fragrant.
4. Assemble the Dish. Once the spaghetti squash is cooked and cool enough to handle, use a fork to shred the squash into strands, transferring the strands to the skillet. Toss the spaghetti squash in the skillet with the garlic-infused fat over low heat. Add the pancetta and the egg-cream-cheese mixture, tossing quickly to coat the squash and gently cook the egg without scrambling. Stir in chopped parsley, and season with freshly ground black pepper.

Nutritional Information (Per Serving):

Calories: 450 kcal | Protein: 18 g | Carbohydrates: 10 g
Fats: 35 g | Cholesterol: 190 mg | Sodium: 700 mg
Potassium: 300 mg

Pork Chops with Mushroom Gravy

 Yield: 4 servings | **Preparation Time:** 15 minutes | **Cooking Time:** 25 minutes

Ingredients:

- 4 bone-in pork chops (about 1 inch thick)
- Salt and black pepper, to taste
- 2 tablespoons olive oil
- 1 tablespoon unsalted butter
- 8 ounces mushrooms, sliced
- 2 cloves garlic, minced
- 1/2 cup chicken broth
- 1 cup heavy cream
- 1 teaspoon Dijon mustard
- 1 teaspoon Worcestershire sauce
- 1/2 teaspoon dried thyme
- Fresh parsley, chopped (for garnish)

Instructions:

1. Prepare the Pork Chops. Pat the pork chops dry with paper towels and season generously with salt and pepper. Heat olive oil in a large skillet over medium-high heat. Add pork chops and sear until golden brown on both sides, about 4-5 minutes per side. Remove pork chops from the skillet and set aside.
2. Make the Mushroom Gravy. In the same skillet, add butter and mushrooms. Sauté until the mushrooms are golden and their moisture has evaporated, about 5-7 minutes. Stir in minced garlic and cook until fragrant, about 1 minute. Pour in chicken broth to deglaze the pan, scraping up any browned bits. Add heavy cream, Dijon mustard, Worcestershire sauce, and thyme. Stir to combine and bring to a simmer. Reduce heat and let the gravy simmer until it thickens, about 5 minutes. Season with salt, pepper, and optional smoked paprika.
3. Combine and Serve. Add the pork chops back to the skillet, spooning the gravy over them. Cover and cook on low heat for another 5-7 minutes, or until the pork chops are cooked through. Garnish with chopped parsley before serving.

Nutritional Information (Per Serving):

Calories: 550 kcal | Protein: 32 g | Carbohydrates: 5 g
Fats: 45 g | Cholesterol: 145 mg | Sodium: 350 mg
Potassium: 650 mg

Eggplant and Beef Layered Casserole

 Yield:
6 servings | Preparation Time:
20 minutes | Cooking Time:
45 minutes

Ingredients:

- 2 medium eggplants, sliced into 1/2-inch thick rounds
- Salt, to draw out moisture from eggplant
- 3 tablespoons olive oil
- 1 pound ground beef
- 1 medium onion, chopped
- 2 cloves garlic, minced
- 1 teaspoon salt
- 1/2 teaspoon black pepper
- 1 cup sugar-free tomato sauce
- 1 teaspoon dried oregano
- 1 teaspoon dried basil
- 1/2 cup heavy cream
- 2 large eggs
- 1 cup shredded mozzarella cheese
- 1/2 cup grated Parmesan cheese

Instructions:

1. Prepare the Eggplant. Lay the eggplant slices on paper towels, sprinkle salt on both sides, and let them sit for about 15 minutes to draw out moisture. Pat dry with paper towels. Preheat the oven to 400°F (200°C). Brush eggplant slices with 2 tablespoons olive oil and place on a baking sheet. Bake for 25 minutes, flipping halfway through until lightly browned and soft.
2. Cook the Beef Mixture. In a skillet, heat 1 tablespoon of olive oil over medium heat. Add the chopped onion and minced garlic, sauté until soft. Add ground beef, salt, and pepper, and cook until browned. Stir in tomato sauce, oregano, and basil. Simmer for 10 minutes, letting the flavors meld.
3. Prepare the Cream Mixture. In a bowl, whisk together heavy cream and eggs. Season with salt and pepper.
4. Assemble the Casserole. In a baking dish, lay half of the baked eggplant slices. Top with half of the beef mixture, then sprinkle with half of the mozzarella and Parmesan cheeses. Repeat the layers. Drizzle the cream and egg mixture over the top layer.
5. Bake the Casserole. Cover with foil and bake in the preheated oven for 20 minutes. Remove foil and bake for another 10 minutes or until the top is golden and bubbly. Let it sit for 10 minutes before serving.

Nutritional Information (Per Serving):

Calories: 450 kcal | Protein: 28 g | Carbohydrates: 12 g
Fats: 34 g | Cholesterol: 160 mg | Sodium: 700 mg
Potassium: 500 mg

Keto Chicken Cacciatore

 Yield:
4 servings | Preparation Time:
15 minutes | Cooking Time:
45 minutes

Ingredients:

- 4 chicken thighs, bone-in and skin-on
- Salt and black pepper, to taste
- 2 tablespoons olive oil
- 1 small onion, finely chopped
- 2 cloves garlic, minced
- 1 bell pepper, sliced
- 1/2 cup sliced mushrooms
- 1 can (14.5 ounces) diced tomatoes, no sugar added
- 1/4 cup chicken broth
- 1 teaspoon dried oregano
- 1 teaspoon dried basil

Instructions:

1. Brown the Chicken. Season chicken thighs generously with salt and pepper. In a large skillet, heat olive oil over medium-high heat. Add chicken, skin-side down, and sear until golden brown, about 5 minutes per side. Remove chicken from the skillet and set aside.
2. Sauté Vegetables. In the same skillet, add onion and garlic, cooking until onion becomes translucent, about 3 minutes. Add bell pepper and mushrooms, sautéing until they start to soften, about 5 minutes.
3. Simmer with Sauce. Stir in diced tomatoes, chicken broth, oregano, basil, and optional red pepper flakes. Bring to a simmer. Return chicken to the skillet, spooning the sauce over the thighs. Cover and simmer on low heat for 30 minutes, until chicken is cooked through.
4. Garnish and Serve: Garnish with fresh chopped parsley before serving.

Nutritional Information (Per Serving):

Calories: 350 kcal | Protein: 25 g | Carbohydrates: 8 g
Fats: 24 g | Cholesterol: 140 mg | Sodium: 300 mg
Potassium: 500 mg

Baked Tilapia with Lemon Butter

 Yield: 4 servings 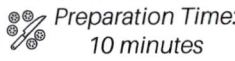 Preparation Time: 10 minutes Cooking Time: 15 minutes

Ingredients:

- 4 tilapia fillets (about 6 ounces each)
- Salt and pepper, to taste
- 4 tablespoons unsalted butter
- 1 lemon, juiced
- 2 cloves garlic, minced
- 1 teaspoon dried parsley
- Additional lemon slices, for garnish
- Fresh dill, chopped (for garnish)

Instructions:

1. Prepare the Fish. Preheat your oven to 400°F (200°C). Pat the tilapia fillets dry with paper towels. Season both sides with salt, pepper, and optional paprika.
2. Make Lemon Butter Sauce. In a small saucepan, melt butter over medium heat. Stir in minced garlic and cook for about 1 minute until fragrant. Remove from heat and stir in lemon juice and dried parsley.
3. Bake the Tilapia. Lightly grease a baking dish with a bit of butter or olive oil. Place the seasoned tilapia fillets in the baking dish. Pour the lemon butter sauce evenly over the fillets. Place in the oven and bake for 12-15 minutes, or until the fish flakes easily with a fork.
4. Garnish and Serve. Garnish with fresh dill and additional lemon slices. Serve hot.

Nutritional Information (Per Serving):

Calories: 240 kcal | Protein: 23 g | Carbohydrates: 1 g
Fats: 16 g | Cholesterol: 75 mg | Sodium: 125 mg
Potassium: 350 mg

Fried Broccoli with Garlic and Shrimp

 Yield: 4 servings 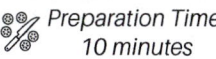 Preparation Time: 10 minutes Cooking Time: 15 minutes

Ingredients:

- 1 lb (450g) large shrimp (peeled and deveined, tails removed)
- 2 cups (200g) broccoli florets
- 3 tbsp olive oil
- 2 tbsp butter (grass-fed, unsalted)
- 4 cloves garlic, minced
- 1 tbsp soy sauce (or coconut aminos for a lower-carb option)
- 1 tbsp lemon juice (optional, for brightness)
- Salt and pepper, to taste
- Fresh parsley or cilantro, chopped, for garnish (optional)

Instructions:

1. Prepare the Ingredients: Ensure the shrimp is peeled and deveined, and the broccoli is cut into bite-sized florets. Mince the garlic and have all ingredients ready for quick cooking.
2. Blanch the Broccoli: Bring a pot of salted water to a boil. Add the broccoli florets and cook for 2 minutes until they turn bright green. Drain and transfer the broccoli to an ice bath (or rinse with cold water) to stop the cooking process. Set aside.
3. In a large skillet, heat 1 tablespoon of olive oil over medium-high heat. Add the shrimp to the skillet in a single layer, season with salt and pepper, and cook for about 1-2 minutes per side until the shrimp are pink and opaque. Remove from the skillet and set aside.
4. In the same skillet, reduce the heat to medium. Add the remaining olive oil and 2 tablespoons of butter. Once the butter has melted, add the minced garlic and sauté for 1 minute until fragrant (but not browned). Add the blanched broccoli florets, season with a pinch of salt, pepper, and red pepper flakes (if using). Stir-fry the broccoli for 3-4 minutes until it's slightly crispy on the edges.
5. Return the cooked shrimp to the skillet, toss to combine with the broccoli and garlic. Add soy sauce or coconut aminos and lemon juice (if using), stir for 1 minute to coat everything evenly. Taste and adjust seasoning if necessary. Garnish with fresh parsley or cilantro.

Nutritional Information (Per Serving):

Calories: 280 kcal | Protein: 24g | Carbohydrates: 5g
Fat: 18g | Cholesterol: 220mg | Sodium: 640mg
Potassium: 470mg

Cauliflower Crust Pizza with Mozzarella and Pepperoni

 Yield: 4 servings   **Preparation Time:** 20 minutes  **Cooking Time:** 30 minutes

Ingredients:

For the Crust:
- 1 large head of cauliflower, riced (about 4 cups)
- 1/4 cup almond flour
- 1/2 cup shredded mozzarella cheese
- 1/4 cup grated Parmesan cheese
- 1 egg
- 1 teaspoon garlic powder
- 1/2 teaspoon salt

For the Topping:
- 1/2 cup low-carb pizza sauce (sugar-free)
- 1 cup shredded mozzarella cheese
- 1/2 cup pepperoni slices
- 1 teaspoon oregano

Instructions:

1. Prepare the Cauliflower Crust. Pulse cauliflower in a food processor until it resembles fine grains. Microwave the riced cauliflower for 8 minutes, then allow to cool. Wrap cooled cauliflower in a clean dish towel and squeeze to remove as much moisture as possible. In a bowl, combine the drained cauliflower with almond flour, shredded mozzarella, Parmesan, egg, garlic powder, and salt. Mix until well combined.
2. Form and Pre-Bake the Crust. Heat your oven to 425°F (220°C). Press the cauliflower mixture onto a baking sheet lined with parchment paper, forming a round shape about 1/4 inch thick. Place in the oven and bake for 15 minutes until the edges are golden and crispy.
3. Add Toppings and Bake. Spread pizza sauce over the baked crust. Top with mozzarella cheese, pepperoni, and sprinkle with oregano. Return to the oven and bake for another 15 minutes, or until the cheese is bubbly and slightly golden.
4. Serve: Slice and serve hot.

Nutritional Information (Per Serving):

Calories: 300 kcal | Protein: 18 g | Carbohydrates: 8 g
Fats: 22 g | Cholesterol: 90 mg | Sodium: 680 mg
Potassium: 300 mg

Lamb Chops with Mint Pesto

 Yield: 4 servings   **Preparation Time:** 15 minutes   **Cooking Time:** 15 minutes

Ingredients:
- 8 lamb chops
- Salt and pepper, to taste
- 2 tablespoons olive oil

For the Mint Pesto:
- 1 cup fresh mint leaves
- 1/2 cup fresh parsley leaves
- 1/4 cup walnuts, toasted
- 2 cloves garlic, minced
- 1/3 cup olive oil
- 2 tablespoons grated Parmesan cheese
- Salt and pepper, to taste

Instructions:

1. Prepare the Mint Pesto. In a food processor, combine mint leaves, parsley, toasted walnuts, and garlic. Pulse until coarsely chopped. While the processor is running, slowly add olive oil until the mixture becomes smooth. Stir in Parmesan cheese, and season with salt and pepper to taste. Add lemon juice if using, for extra zest.
2. Cook the Lamb Chops. Season the lamb chops generously with salt and pepper. In a large skillet, heat olive oil over medium-high heat. Add lamb chops to the skillet, cooking each side for about 3-4 minutes for medium-rare, or longer depending on your desired doneness.
3. Serve. Arrange the lamb chops on plates. Spoon mint pesto over the lamb chops.

Nutritional Information (Per Serving):

Calories: 450 kcal | Protein: 28 g | Carbohydrates: 2 g
Fats: 37 g | Cholesterol: 105 mg | Sodium: 200 mg
Potassium: 400 mg

Cod in Creamy Red Roasted Pepper Sauce

 Yield:
4 servings
 Preparation Time:
15 minutes
 Cooking Time:
25 minutes

Ingredients:

- 4 cod fillets (about 6 ounces each)
- Salt and black pepper, to taste
- 2 tablespoons olive oil
- 1 medium onion, finely chopped
- 3 cloves garlic, minced
- 1 cup roasted red peppers, drained and chopped
- 1 cup heavy cream
- 1/2 cup grated Parmesan cheese
- 1 tablespoon fresh basil, chopped
- 1 teaspoon smoked paprika
- 1/2 lemon, juiced

Instructions:

1. Prepare the Cod. Pat the cod fillets dry with paper towels and season both sides with salt and black pepper. Heat olive oil in a large skillet over medium-high heat. Add the cod fillets and cook for about 4-5 minutes on each side or until cooked through and easily flaked with a fork. Remove from the skillet and set aside.
2. Make the Sauce. In the same skillet, add the chopped onion and cook until translucent, about 3-4 minutes. Add the garlic and cook for an additional 1 minute until fragrant. Stir in the chopped roasted red peppers and smoked paprika, cooking for another 2 minutes. Pour in the heavy cream and bring the mixture to a simmer. Let it cook for 5 minutes, then stir in the grated Parmesan cheese until the sauce is creamy and cheese is melted. Mix in the fresh basil and lemon juice, then season with salt and pepper to taste.
3. Combine and Serve. Return the cod fillets to the skillet, spooning the sauce over them. Let simmer for another 2-3 minutes to ensure the fish is heated through and infused with the sauce.
4. Serve immediately.

Nutritional Information (Per Serving):

Calories: 450 | Protein: 36g | Carbohydrates: 8g
Fats: 32g | Cholesterol: 120mg | Sodium: 320mg
Potassium: 650mg

Roast Turkey with Low-Carb Gravy

 Yield:
8 servings
Preparation Time:
30 minutes
 Cooking Time:
3 hours

Ingredients:

For the Turkey:
- 1 whole turkey (about 12-14 pounds), thawed and giblets removed
- 1/4 cup olive oil
- 2 tablespoons butter, softened
- 4 garlic cloves, minced
- 1 lemon, halved
- 2 onions, quartered
- 2 carrots, cut into chunks
- 2 celery stalks, cut into chunks
- Salt and pepper, to taste

For the Low-Carb Gravy:
- Pan drippings from the roast turkey
- 2 cups chicken or turkey broth
- 1/4 cup cream
- 2 teaspoons xanthan gum
- Salt and pepper, to taste

Instructions:

1. Preheat your oven to 325°F (165°C). Pat the turkey dry with paper towels. Rub the outside and cavity of the turkey with olive oil and butter, and season generously with salt, pepper, and minced garlic. Stuff the cavity with lemon halves, one onion quartered, a few carrot and celery chunks, and fresh herbs.
2. Place the turkey breast side up in a roasting pan. Arrange the remaining onions, carrots, celery. Tent the turkey with aluminum foil and roast in the preheated oven. Cooking time is about 13 minutes per pound. For a 14-pound turkey, this will be approximately 3 hours. Remove the foil in the last 30 minutes to brown the skin.
3. Make the Low-Carb Gravy: Once the turkey is done, transfer it to a cutting board to rest. Pour the pan drippings into a saucepan. Skim off the excess fat. Add chicken or turkey broth to the drippings and bring to a simmer. Dissolve xanthan gum in a small amount of cold water and whisk into the simmering liquid. Stir in the cream and continue to simmer until the gravy thickens. Season with salt and pepper.
4. Carve the turkey and serve with the low-carb gravy.

Nutritional Information (Per Serving):

Calories: 570 | Protein: 70 g | Carbohydrates: 5 g
Fats: 30 g | Cholesterol: 185 mg | Sodium: 340 mg
Potassium: 690 mg

Garlic Parmesan Chicken Wings

 Yield:
4 servings

 Preparation Time:
10 minutes

 Cooking Time:
45 minutes

Ingredients:

- 2 pounds chicken wings, tips removed, drumettes and flats separated
- 1 tablespoon baking powder (aluminum-free)
- 1/2 teaspoon salt
- 1/4 teaspoon black pepper
- 1/2 cup butter
- 4 cloves garlic, minced
- 1/2 cup grated Parmesan cheese
- 2 tablespoons fresh parsley, chopped

Instructions:

1. Prepare the Wings: Pat the chicken wings dry with paper towels. This helps achieve a crispy skin. In a large bowl, mix the baking powder, salt, and pepper. Toss the wings in the mixture until evenly coated.
2. Bake the Wings: Preheat your oven to 400°F (200°C). Line a baking sheet with parchment paper and place a wire rack on top. Arrange the wings on the wire rack in a single layer. Bake for about 40 minutes or until golden and crisp, flipping halfway through.
3. Make the Garlic Parmesan Sauce: While the wings are baking, melt the butter in a small saucepan over medium heat. Add the minced garlic and cook for 1-2 minutes until fragrant but not browned. Remove from heat and stir in the grated Parmesan cheese.
4. Toss the Wings: Once the wings are cooked and crispy, remove them from the oven and place them in a large bowl. Pour the garlic Parmesan sauce over the wings and toss to coat evenly. Sprinkle with chopped parsley.
5. Serve the wings hot with your choice of keto-friendly sides or dips.

Nutritional Information (Per Serving):

Calories: 540 | Protein: 38 g | Carbohydrates: 3 g
Fats: 42 g | Cholesterol: 185 mg | Sodium: 650 mg
Potassium: 300 mg

Pan-Seared Duck Breast with Red Wine Sauce

Yield:
2 servings

Preparation Time:
15 minutes

Cooking Time:
30 minutes

Ingredients:

- 2 duck breasts (approximately 6-8 oz each)
- Salt and black pepper, to taste
- 1/2 cup dry red wine (choose a low-carb option)
- 1/4 cup chicken broth, low sodium
- 1 tablespoon unsalted butter
- 1 clove garlic, minced
- 1 sprig fresh thyme

Instructions:

1. Prepare the Duck: Score the skin of the duck breasts in a diamond pattern, being careful not to cut into the flesh. Season both sides with salt and pepper. Place the duck breasts skin-side down in a cold non-stick skillet. Turn the heat to medium and cook for about 6-8 minutes, or until the skin is crispy and golden.
2. Cook the Duck: Flip the duck breasts over and cook for an additional 4-6 minutes for medium-rare (adjust time for desired doneness). Remove the duck from the skillet and let it rest.
3. Make the Red Wine Sauce: Pour off most of the fat from the skillet, leaving about a tablespoon behind. Add the minced garlic and thyme sprig; sauté for about 1 minute until fragrant. Deglaze the skillet with red wine, scraping up any browned bits from the bottom. Add chicken broth and simmer until the sauce is reduced by half, about 8-10 minutes. Remove from heat, discard the thyme sprig, and whisk in the butter until the sauce is glossy and slightly thickened.
4. Slice and Serve: Slice the duck breasts thinly. Drizzle the red wine sauce over the slices.

Nutritional Information (Per Serving):

Calories: 560 | Protein: 45 g | Carbohydrates: 3 g
Fats: 40 g | Cholesterol: 155 mg | Sodium: 220 mg
Potassium: 595 mg

Beef and Broccoli Stir-Fry

 Yield:
4 servings   Preparation Time:
15 minutes   Cooking Time:
10 minutes

Ingredients:

- 1 pound beef sirloin, thinly sliced against the grain
- 3 cups broccoli florets
- 2 tablespoons coconut oil
- 1 tablespoon ginger, minced
- 2 cloves garlic, minced
- 1/4 cup soy sauce (or coconut aminos for a soy-free option)
- 1 tablespoon sesame oil
- 1/2 cup beef broth
- Salt and pepper, to taste

Instructions:

1. Prepare Ingredient: Wash and cut broccoli into florets. Mince garlic and ginger. Slice the beef into thin strips, if not already prepped.
2. Stir-Fry Beef: Heat 1 tablespoon of coconut oil in a large skillet or wok over high heat. Add the beef in a single layer, allowing it to sear without stirring initially, about 1-2 minutes. Then stir-fry until browned and nearly cooked through. Remove beef from the skillet and set aside.
3. Cook Broccoli: n the same skillet, add another tablespoon of coconut oil. Add the broccoli, ginger, and garlic, stir-frying for about 3-4 minutes until the broccoli is tender but still crisp.
4. Make the Sauce: Lower the heat to medium. Return the beef to the skillet with the broccoli. Pour in the soy sauce (or coconut aminos), beef broth, and sesame oil. Season with salt, pepper, and optional red pepper flakes. Stir well to combine and thicken the sauce.
5. Combine and Serve: Cook together for an additional 2-3 minutes, allowing the flavors to meld. Adjust seasoning as needed.

Nutritional Information (Per Serving):

Calories: 300 | Protein: 26 g | Carbohydrates: 8 g
Fats: 18 g | Cholesterol: 55 mg | Sodium: 800 mg
Potassium: 500 mg

SNACKS & APPETIZERS

Perfect picks for between meals or small gatherings

Keto Nachos

 Yield: 4 servings   **Preparation Time:** 10 minutes   **Cooking Time:** 10 minutes

Ingredients:
- 2 cups pepperoni slices (choose larger, thin slices for best results)
- 1 cup shredded cheddar cheese
- 1/2 cup diced bell peppers
- 1/2 cup black olives, sliced
- 1/4 cup red onion, finely chopped
- 1/2 cup sour cream
- 1/4 cup guacamole
- 1/4 cup salsa (check for no added sugar)

Instructions:
1. Prepare Pepperoni Chips: Preheat the oven to 400°F (200°C). Arrange pepperoni slices in a single layer on a baking sheet lined with parchment paper. Bake for 8-10 minutes until crisp. Remove from oven and let cool slightly—they will crisp up as they cool.
2. Assemble the Nachos: Once pepperoni chips have cooled, arrange them on an oven-proof platter or baking sheet. Sprinkle evenly with shredded cheddar cheese, diced bell peppers, black olives, red onion. Place the platter back in the oven for about 3-5 minutes, or until the cheese is fully melted.
3. Add Toppings: Remove from the oven and immediately add dollops of sour cream, guacamole, and salsa over the top.

Nutritional Information (Per Serving):
Calories: 480 | Protein: 25 g | Carbohydrates: 6 g
Fats: 40 g | Cholesterol: 100 mg | Sodium: 1380 mg
Potassium: 350 mg

Bacon Avocado Bombs

Yield: 4 servings   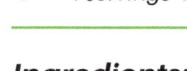 **Preparation Time:** 10 minutes   **Cooking Time:** 15 minutes

Ingredients:
- 2 large avocados
- 8 slices of bacon
- 1/2 cup cream cheese, softened
- 1 tablespoon lime juice
- 1/4 teaspoon garlic powder
- 1/4 teaspoon onion powder
- Salt and pepper, to taste

Instructions:
1. Prepare the Avocado Mixture: Cut the avocados in half and remove the pits. Scoop out some of the flesh to make room for the filling, leaving a thick shell of avocado. In a bowl, mash the scooped avocado with lime juice, garlic powder, onion powder, salt, and pepper. Mix in the cream cheese until well combined.
2. Stuff the Avocado: Fill the hollowed-out avocado halves with the cream cheese mixture, smoothing the tops.
3. Wrap with Bacon: Wrap each stuffed avocado half with 2 slices of bacon. Ensure the bacon overlaps slightly and covers the entire avocado. Secure with toothpicks if necessary.
4. Bake the Avocado Bombs: Preheat the oven to 400°F (200°C). Place the bacon-wrapped avocados on a baking sheet lined with parchment paper. Bake in the preheated oven for 15 minutes or until the bacon is crispy and golden.
5. Serve: Remove from the oven, let cool slightly.

Nutritional Information (Per Serving):
Calories: 350 | Protein: 12 g | Carbohydrates: 9 g
Fats: 30 g | Cholesterol: 45 mg | Sodium: 480 mg
Potassium: 640 mg

Cauliflower Hummus

 Yield:
6 servings
Preparation Time:
10 minutes
Cooking Time:
20 minutes

Ingredients:
- 1 large head cauliflower, cut into florets
- 1/4 cup tahini
- 2 tablespoons olive oil, plus more for garnish
- 2 cloves garlic, minced
- Juice of 1 lemon
- 1 teaspoon ground cumin
- Salt and pepper, to taste
- Optional for garnish: Paprika, chopped parsley, additional olive oil

Instructions:
1. Cook the Cauliflower: Preheat the oven to 400°F (200°C). Spread cauliflower florets on a baking sheet and drizzle with 1 tablespoon of olive oil. Season with salt and pepper. Roast in the preheated oven for about 20 minutes or until tender and slightly golden. Remove and let cool slightly.
2. Blend the Hummus: In a food processor, combine the roasted cauliflower, tahini, remaining 1 tablespoon of olive oil, minced garlic, lemon juice, and cumin. Process until smooth. If the mixture is too thick, add a little water to reach your desired consistency. Season with salt and pepper to taste.
3. Garnish and Serve: Transfer the hummus to a serving bowl. Drizzle with additional olive oil and sprinkle with paprika and chopped parsley for garnish.

Nutritional Information (Per Serving):
Calories: 140 | Protein: 4 g | Carbohydrates: 8 g
Fats: 11 g | Cholesterol: 0 mg | Sodium: 30 mg
Potassium: 360 mg

Cheese and Herb Stuffed Mushrooms

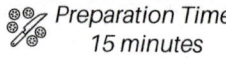 Yield:
4 servings
 Preparation Time:
15 minutes
Cooking Time:
20 minutes

Ingredients:
- 12 large cremini or white mushrooms
- 1/4 cup cream cheese, softened
- 1/4 cup grated Parmesan cheese
- 2 tablespoons unsalted butter
- 2 cloves garlic, minced
- 1 tablespoon fresh thyme, chopped
- 1 tablespoon fresh parsley, chopped
- Salt and pepper, to taste

Instructions:
1. Preheat your oven to 375°F (190°C).
2. Prepare the Mushroom Caps: Gently clean the mushroom caps with a damp towel. Scoop out a little from the inside of each cap to create more space for the filling.
3. Cook the Mushroom Stems: In a skillet over medium heat, melt butter. Add the chopped mushroom stems and garlic, cooking until they are soft and browned, about 5-7 minutes. Remove from heat and let cool slightly.
4. Prepare the Filling: In a mixing bowl, combine the cooked mushroom stems and garlic, cream cheese, Parmesan cheese, thyme, and parsley. Season with salt and pepper to taste. Mix until well combined.
5. Stuff the Mushrooms: Spoon the cheese and herb mixture into each mushroom cap, filling them generously.
6. Bake the Stuffed Mushrooms: Arrange the stuffed mushrooms on a baking sheet. Bake in the preheated oven for 20 minutes, or until the mushrooms are tender and the tops are golden brown.

Nutritional Information (Per Serving):
Calories: 180 | Protein: 7 g | Carbohydrates: 5 g
Fats: 15 g | Cholesterol: 30 mg | Sodium: 200 mg
Potassium: 300 mg

Keto-Friendly Stuffed Bell Peppers

 Yield:
4 servings | Preparation Time:
20 minutes | Cooking Time:
30 minutes

Ingredients:

- 4 large bell peppers (any color), tops cut off and seeds removed
- 1 pound ground beef (85% lean)
- 1 cup cauliflower rice
- 1/2 cup onion, finely chopped
- 2 cloves garlic, minced
- 1 cup shredded cheddar cheese
- 1/4 cup cream cheese
- 1 tablespoon olive oil
- 1 teaspoon smoked paprika
- 1 teaspoon cumin
- Salt and pepper, to taste

Instructions:

1. Preheat your oven to 375°F (190°C).
2. Prepare the bell peppers by slicing off the tops and removing the seeds and membranes. Set aside.
3. Cook the Filling: Heat olive oil in a skillet over medium heat. Add the chopped onion and garlic, sautéing until translucent and fragrant. Add the ground beef, breaking it up with a spoon, and cook until browned. Stir in the cauliflower rice, smoked paprika, cumin, salt, and pepper. Cook for another 5 minutes until everything is well combined. Remove from heat and mix in the cream cheese and half of the cheddar cheese until melted and blended.
4. Stuff the Peppers: Spoon the beef and cauliflower mixture into each bell pepper. Place the stuffed peppers in a baking dish.
5. Bake the Peppers: Sprinkle the remaining cheddar cheese over the top of each stuffed pepper. Bake in the preheated oven for 30 minutes, or until the peppers are tender and the cheese is bubbly and golden.

Nutritional Information (Per Serving):

Calories: 450 | Protein: 28 g | Carbohydrates: 12 g
Fats: 32 g | Cholesterol: 100 mg | Sodium: 320 mg
Potassium: 650 mg

Spring Rolls

Yield:
6 servings
(2 rolls per serving) | Preparation Time:
30 minutes | Cooking Time:
5 minutes

Ingredients:

For the Rolls:
- 12 large cabbage leaves, blanched and dried
- 1-pound cooked shrimp, peeled and sliced in half lengthwise
- 1 large avocado, thinly sliced
- 1 cucumber, julienned
- 1/2 cup fresh cilantro leaves
- 1/2 cup fresh mint leaves

For the Dipping Sauce:
- 1/4 cup almond butter
- 2 tablespoons soy sauce (or coconut aminos for a soy-free version)
- 1 tablespoon lime juice
- 1 tablespoon erythritol (or another keto-friendly sweetener)
- 1 teaspoon chili paste (adjust to taste)
- Water, as needed to thin the sauce

Instructions:

1. Prepare the Cabbage Leaves: Bring a large pot of water to a boil. Blanch the cabbage leaves for about 30 seconds or until pliable. Immediately transfer them to an ice bath to stop the cooking process. Pat dry and trim the tough central rib from each leaf to facilitate easier rolling.
2. Make the Dipping Sauce: In a small bowl, whisk together almond butter, soy sauce, lime juice, erythritol, and chili paste. Add water a tablespoon at a time until you reach a desired consistency for dipping.
3. Assemble the Spring Rolls: Lay a cabbage leaf flat on a cutting board. Place a few pieces of shrimp, a couple of slices of avocado, a few sticks of cucumber on the leaf. Add a few cilantro and mint leaves on top of the vegetables. Fold the bottom half of the cabbage leaf over the filling, then fold in the sides and roll tightly. Repeat with the remaining ingredients.
4. Serve: Cut each roll in half diagonally and serve with the dipping sauce.

Nutritional Information (Per Serving):

Calories: 250 | Protein: 20 g | Carbohydrates: 8 g
Fats: 16 g | Cholesterol: 120 mg | Sodium: 300 mg
Potassium: 400 mg

Bacon-Wrapped Asparagus

 Yield: 4 servings   **Preparation Time:** 10 minutes   **Cooking Time:** 20 minutes

Ingredients:

- 16 asparagus spears, trimmed
- 8 slices of thick-cut bacon
- 1 tablespoon olive oil
- Salt and pepper, to taste
- Optional: 1 tablespoon Parmesan cheese, grated
- Optional: 1 teaspoon garlic powder

Instructions:

1. Preheat your oven to 400°F (200°C).
2. Prepare the Asparagus: Wash and trim the tough ends of the asparagus spears. Pat dry.
3. Season and Wrap: Lightly coat the asparagus spears with olive oil, salt, and pepper. Optionally sprinkle with garlic powder for extra flavor. Cut the bacon strips in half, crosswise. Wrap each piece of bacon tightly around an asparagus spear in a spiral. Secure the bacon with toothpicks if necessary.
4. Bake: Arrange the bacon-wrapped asparagus on a baking sheet lined with parchment paper or a silicone mat. Bake in the preheated oven for about 20 minutes, or until the bacon is crisp and the asparagus is tender. For extra crispiness, broil for the last 2-3 minutes.
5. Finish and Serve: Remove from the oven and optionally sprinkle with grated Parmesan cheese while still hot.

Nutritional Information (Per Serving):

Calories: 220 | Protein: 10 g | Carbohydrates: 3 g
Fats: 20 g | Cholesterol: 30 mg | Sodium: 320 mg
Potassium: 230 mg

Garlic Cheese Bread Sticks

Yield: 4 servings   **Preparation Time:** 15 minutes   **Cooking Time:** 20 minutes

Ingredients:

- 1 1/2 cups shredded mozzarella cheese
- 2 tablespoons cream cheese
- 1 cup almond flour
- 1 teaspoon baking powder
- 1 large egg
- 2 cloves garlic, minced
- 1/2 teaspoon garlic powder
- 1/2 teaspoon salt
- 1/4 cup grated Parmesan cheese
- 2 tablespoons unsalted butter, melted

Instructions:

1. Preheat your oven to 375°F (190°C). Line a baking sheet with parchment paper or a silicone baking mat.
2. Make the Dough: In a microwave-safe bowl, combine the mozzarella cheese and cream cheese. Microwave for about 1 minute or until the cheeses are completely melted and can be stirred together smoothly. Stir in the almond flour, baking powder, and egg to the melted cheese mixture, mixing until a dough forms.
3. Shape the Bread Sticks: Place the dough onto the prepared baking sheet. Wet your hands slightly to prevent sticking and press the dough into a rectangular shape, about 1/2 inch thick. In a small bowl, mix the minced garlic, garlic powder, and melted butter. Brush this mixture over the top of the dough. Sprinkle the grated Parmesan cheese evenly over the top.
4. Bake in the preheated oven for about 15-20 minutes, or until golden brown and firm.
5. Serve: Remove from the oven. Cut into sticks and serve warm.

Nutritional Information (Per Serving):

Calories: 380 | Protein: 20 g | Carbohydrates: 6 g
Fats: 32 g | Cholesterol: 110 mg | Sodium: 560 mg
Potassium: 200 mg

Salmon and Cream Cheese Bites

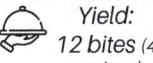 **Yield:**
12 bites (4 servings)

 Preparation Time:
15 minutes

Cooking Time:
0 minutes (no cook, assembly only)

Ingredients:
- 6 ounces smoked salmon, sliced into bite-sized pieces
- 4 ounces cream cheese, softened
- 1 tablespoon fresh dill, chopped
- 1 tablespoon capers, drained
- 1 teaspoon lemon zest
- 1 tablespoon lemon juice
- Black pepper, to taste
- 12 cucumber slices, about 1/4-inch thick

Optional for garnish:
- Extra dill for topping
- Red onion slices, very thin

Instructions:
1. Prepare the Cream Cheese Mixture. In a small bowl, combine the softened cream cheese, chopped dill, capers, lemon zest, and lemon juice. Mix until smooth and well combined. Season with black pepper to taste.
2. Assemble the Bites. Lay out the cucumber slices on a serving tray. These will serve as the crunchy base for the bites. Spoon or pipe a small amount of the cream cheese mixture onto each cucumber slice. Top each cream cheese-topped cucumber slice with a piece of smoked salmon.
3. Garnish: If desired, add a small sprig of dill or a thin slice of red onion on top for extra flavor and decoration.

Nutritional Information (Per Serving):
Calories: 150 kcal | Protein: 10 g | Carbohydrates: 2 g
Fats: 12 g | Cholesterol: 35 mg | Sodium: 600 mg
Potassium: 200 mg

Keto Mini Pizzas

 Yield:
6 servings

 Preparation Time:
15 minutes

Cooking Time:
15 minutes

(2 mini pizzas per serving)

Ingredients:
For the Crust:
- 1 1/2 cups mozzarella cheese, shredded
- 2 tablespoons cream cheese
- 3/4 cup almond flour
- 1 egg
- 1/2 teaspoon garlic powder
- 1/2 teaspoon oregano

For the Toppings:
- 1/2 cup low-carb pizza sauce
- 1 cup mozzarella cheese, shredded
- 1/2 cup cooked sausage, crumbled
- 1/4 cup pepperoni slices
- 1/4 cup green bell pepper, diced
- 1/4 cup mushrooms, sliced

Instructions:
1. Prepare the Dough: Preheat your oven to 425°F (220°C) and line a baking sheet with parchment paper. In a microwave-safe bowl, combine 1 1/2 cups mozzarella and cream cheese. Microwave for about 60 seconds or until the cheeses are melted and can be mixed. Stir in almond flour, egg, garlic powder, and oregano until a dough forms.
2. Shape the Mini Pizzas: Divide the dough into 12 equal parts. Roll each piece into a ball, then flatten on the prepared baking sheet to form mini pizza bases, about 4 inches in diameter.
3. Pre-Bake the Crusts: Bake the mini crusts for 6-8 minutes, or until they begin to turn golden. Remove from the oven.
4. Add Toppings: Spread a tablespoon of pizza sauce on each mini crust. Sprinkle with mozzarella, then add sausage, pepperoni, bell peppers, and mushrooms.
5. Bake the Mini Pizzas: Return the pizzas to the oven and bake for another 7-10 minutes, or until the cheese is bubbly and the edges are crisp.

Nutritional Information (Per Serving):
Calories: 380 | Protein: 22 g | Carbohydrates: 6 g
Fats: 30 g | Cholesterol: 95 mg | Sodium: 540 mg
Potassium: 200 mg

Baked Avocado Fries

Yield: 4 servings | **Preparation Time:** 10 minutes | **Cooking Time:** 15 minutes

Ingredients:

- 2 large ripe but firm avocados
- 1 cup almond flour
- 1 teaspoon garlic powder
- 1 teaspoon paprika
- Salt and pepper, to taste
- 2 large eggs, beaten
- Optional for dipping: Spicy mayo or keto-friendly ranch dressing

Instructions:

1. Preheat your oven to 400°F (200°C). Line a baking sheet with parchment paper or a silicone baking mat.
2. Prepare the Avocados: Cut the avocados in half, remove the pits, and peel off the skin. Slice each half into 6-8 wedges depending on the size of the avocado.
3. Prepare the Coating: In a shallow bowl, mix almond flour, garlic powder, paprika, salt, and pepper. Place the beaten eggs in another shallow bowl.
4. Coat the Avocado Slices: Dip each avocado slice first in the beaten egg, then roll it in the almond flour mixture until well coated. Arrange the coated avocado slices on the prepared baking sheet.
5. Bake the Avocado Fries: Bake in the preheated oven for about 15 minutes or until the coating is golden and crispy. Turn the slices halfway through the baking time to ensure even cooking.
6. Serve the avocado fries hot with a side of spicy mayo or keto-friendly ranch dressing for dipping.

Nutritional Information (Per Serving):

Calories: 320 | Protein: 8 g | Carbohydrates: 12 g
Fats: 27 g | Cholesterol: 93 mg | Sodium: 120 mg
Potassium: 540 mg

DESSERTS

Sweet treats without the sugar spike.

Chocolate Chip Cookies

🛎 **Yield:** 12 servings ✳ **Preparation Time:** 10 minutes 🍲 **Cooking Time:** 12 minutes

Ingredients:

- 1 1/2 cups almond flour
- 1/4 cup coconut flour
- 1/2 teaspoon baking soda
- 1/4 teaspoon salt
- 1/2 cup unsalted butter, softened
- 3/4 cup erythritol
- 1 large egg
- 1 teaspoon vanilla extract
- 1/2 cup sugar-free chocolate chips
- 1/2 cup chopped walnuts or pecans

Instructions:

1. Preheat your oven to 350°F (175°C). Line a baking sheet with parchment paper.
2. Mix Dry Ingredients: In a medium bowl, whisk together almond flour, coconut flour, baking soda, and salt.
3. Cream Butter and Sweetener: In a large bowl, use an electric mixer to cream together the butter and erythritol until light and fluffy. Beat in the egg and vanilla extract until well combined.
4. Combine with Dry Ingredients: Gradually add the dry ingredients to the wet ingredients, mixing until just combined.
5. Fold in the sugar-free chocolate chips and nuts.
6. Form Cookies: Scoop tablespoon-sized amounts of dough and roll into balls. Place them on the prepared baking sheet, pressing down slightly to flatten.
7. Bake in the preheated oven for 12 minutes, or until the edges are golden brown.
8. Allow the cookies to cool on the baking sheet for 5 minutes before transferring them to a wire rack to cool completely.

Nutritional Information (Per Serving):

Calories: 180 | Protein: 4 g | Carbohydrates: 6 g
Fats: 16 g | Cholesterol: 20 mg | Sodium: 85 mg
Potassium: 50 mg

Almond Butter Brownies

🛎 **Yield:** 12 servings ✳ **Preparation Time:** 10 minutes 🍲 **Cooking Time:** 20 minutes

Ingredients:

- 1 cup almond butter
- 1/3 cup keto-friendly sweetener
- 1/4 cup unsweetened cocoa powder
- 2 large eggs
- 2 tablespoons coconut oil, melted
- 1 teaspoon vanilla extract
- 1/2 teaspoon baking soda
- 1/4 teaspoon salt
- Optional: 1/4 cup sugar-free chocolate chips or chopped nuts for topping

Instructions:

1. Preheat your oven to 350°F (175°C). Grease an 8x8 inch baking pan or line it with parchment paper for easy removal.
2. In a large mixing bowl, combine the almond butter, eggs, melted coconut oil, and vanilla extract. Mix well until all ingredients are smoothly blended. Add the cocoa powder, sweetener, baking soda, and salt to the wet mixture. Stir until the batter is well combined and no lumps remain. If using, fold in the sugar-free chocolate chips or chopped nuts into the batter to add texture and extra flavor.
3. Pour the batter into the prepared baking pan. Use a spatula to smooth it into an even layer.
4. Bake: Place the pan in the preheated oven and bake for 20 minutes, or until the edges start to pull away from the sides of the pan and a toothpick inserted into the center comes out with few moist crumbs.
5. Cool and Serve: Remove the brownies from the oven and let them cool in the pan for about 10 minutes. Then, lift them out (if using parchment paper) and cut into 12 squares.

Nutritional Information (Per Serving):

Calories: 180 | Protein: 5 g | Carbohydrates: 6 g
Fats: 16 g | Cholesterol: 35 mg | Sodium: 130 mg
Potassium: 200 mg

Coconut Bars

🍽 Yield: 12 servings 🌿 Preparation Time: 10 minutes ⏲ Cooking Time: 20 minutes

Ingredients:
- 1 cup unsweetened shredded coconut
- 1/2 cup almond flour
- 1/4 cup coconut oil, melted
- 1/4 cup unsalted butter, melted
- 1/3 cup erythritol (or another keto-friendly sweetener)
- 1 teaspoon vanilla extract
- 1/4 teaspoon salt
- 2 large eggs
- Optional: 1/4 cup sugar-free chocolate chips for topping

Instructions:
1. Preheat your oven to 350°F (175°C). Line an 8x8 inch baking dish with parchment paper.
2. In a medium mixing bowl, combine the shredded coconut, almond flour, erythritol, and salt. Mix thoroughly to distribute the ingredients evenly. In another bowl, whisk together the melted coconut oil, melted butter, vanilla extract, and eggs until smooth. Pour the wet ingredients into the bowl with the dry ingredients and stir until well combined.
3. Bake: Transfer the mixture to the prepared baking dish, spreading it out evenly. If using, sprinkle the top with sugar-free chocolate chips. Bake in the preheated oven for 20 minutes, or until the edges are golden brown and the center is set.
4. Cool and Cut: Allow the coconut bars to cool completely in the pan on a wire rack. Once cooled, lift the parchment paper to remove the entire block from the pan and cut into 12 even bars.

Nutritional Information (Per Serving):
Calories: 180 | Protein: 3 g | Carbohydrates: 4 g
Fats: 17 g | Cholesterol: 35 mg | Sodium: 55 mg
Potassium: 50 mg

Lemon Curd Tart

🍽 Yield: 8 servings 🌿 Preparation Time: 20 minutes ⏲ Cooking Time: 35 minutes

Ingredients:
For the Crust:
- 1 1/2 cups almond flour
- 1/4 cup coconut flour
- 1/3 cup erythritol
- 1/2 cup unsalted butter, melted
- 1 teaspoon vanilla extract
- Pinch of salt

For the Lemon Curd:
- 1/2 cup lemon juice
- (about 2-3 lemons)
- 1 tablespoon lemon zest
- 1/2 cup erythritol
- 3 large eggs
- 1 egg yolk
- 6 tablespoons unsalted butter, cubed
- Optional garnish: Whipped cream and fresh mint leaves

Instructions:
1. Preheat your oven to 350°F (175°C). In a mixing bowl, combine almond flour, coconut flour, erythritol, melted butter, vanilla extract, and a pinch of salt. Stir until the mixture forms a dough. Press the dough into the bottom and up the sides of a 9-inch tart pan with a removable bottom. Use a measuring cup to smooth the surface. Bake the crust in the preheated oven for 10-12 minutes or until golden. Remove and let cool while you prepare the curd.
2. In a medium saucepan, whisk together lemon juice, lemon zest, erythritol, eggs, and egg yolk. Cook over medium-low heat, stirring constantly, until the mixture thickens (about 10 minutes). Remove the pan from heat and stir in the cubed butter until the mixture is smooth and creamy.
3. Assemble the Tart: Pour the warm lemon curd into the baked tart crust. Use a spatula to smooth the top. Let the tart cool at room temperature, then refrigerate for at least 2-3 hours until set.
4. Garnish with optional whipped cream and fresh mint leaves before serving. Slice and serve chilled.

Nutritional Information (Per Serving):
Calories: 350 | Protein: 7 g | Carbohydrates: 8 g
Fats: 32 g | Cholesterol: 155 mg | Sodium: 85 mg
Potassium: 50 mg

Keto Blueberry Muffins

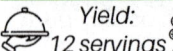 **Yield:** 12 servings  **Preparation Time:** 15 minutes  **Cooking Time:** 20 minutes

Ingredients:

- 2 cups almond flour
- 1/3 cup coconut flour
- 1/2 cup erythritol (or another keto-friendly sweetener)
- 1 teaspoon baking powder
- 1/2 teaspoon salt
- 1/3 cup unsalted butter, melted
- 1/3 cup unsweetened almond milk
- 3 large eggs
- 1 teaspoon vanilla extract
- 1 cup fresh blueberries (or frozen, if fresh are unavailable)

Instructions:

1. Preheat your oven to 350°F (175°C). Line a muffin pan with paper liners or grease the cups with butter or non-stick spray.
2. In a large bowl, whisk together almond flour, coconut flour, erythritol, baking powder, and salt. In another bowl, mix the melted butter, almond milk, eggs, and vanilla extract. Add the wet ingredients to the dry ingredients, stirring until just combined. Do not overmix.
3. Fold in Blueberries: Gently fold the blueberries into the batter to distribute them evenly without crushing.
4. Fill Muffin Cups and Bake: Divide the batter evenly among the prepared muffin cups, filling each about 3/4 full. Bake for 20 minutes, or until the tops are golden and a toothpick inserted into the center of a muffin comes out clean.
5. Cool and Serve: Let the muffins cool in the pan for about 5 minutes, then transfer them to a wire rack to cool completely.

Nutritional Information (Per Serving):

Calories: 180 | Protein: 6 g | Carbohydrates: 7 g (Net Carbs: 3 g) | Fats: 15 g | Fiber: 4 g | Cholesterol: 55 mg Sodium: 125 mg | Potassium: 35 mg

Creamy Panna Cotta

 Yield: 6 servings 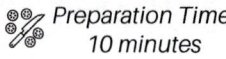 **Preparation Time:** 10 minutes   **Cooking Time:** 4 hours

Ingredients:

- 2 cups heavy cream
- 1/2 cup unsweetened almond milk
- 1/4 cup erythritol or another keto-friendly sweetener
- 1 vanilla bean, split lengthwise and seeds scraped (or 1 teaspoon vanilla extract)
- 2 1/2 teaspoons unflavored gelatin powder
- 3 tablespoons cold water
- Optional for garnish: Fresh berries, mint leaves.

Instructions:

1. Hydrate the Gelatin: In a small bowl, sprinkle the gelatin over the cold water. Let sit for about 5 minutes until the gelatin absorbs the water and becomes gel-like.
2. Heat the Cream Mixture: In a saucepan over medium heat, combine the heavy cream, almond milk, and erythritol. Add the vanilla bean pod and seeds (or vanilla extract). Heat the mixture just until it starts to simmer, then remove from heat. Do not let it boil.
3. Dissolve the Gelatin: Remove the vanilla bean pod if used. Add the hydrated gelatin to the hot cream mixture and stir until the gelatin is completely dissolved.
4. Pour into Molds: Divide the mixture evenly among 6 ramekins or molds. If you want to unmold the panna cotta for serving, lightly grease the ramekins with a neutral oil first.
5. Chill: Refrigerate the panna cotta for at least 4 hours, or until set.
6. Serve: If unmolding, briefly dip the bottom of each ramekin in warm water, then invert onto a serving plate. Garnish with fresh berries and mint leaves.

Nutritional Information (Per Serving):

Calories: 300 | Protein: 3 g | Carbohydrates: 3 g | Fats: 30 g | Cholesterol: 90 mg | Sodium: 50 mg | Potassium: 50 mg

Low-Carb Raspberry Swirl Cheesecake

 Yield: 12 servings

 Preparation Time: 30 minutes

 Cooking Time: 50 minutes

 Chilling Time: 4 hours

Ingredients:

For the Crust:
- 1 1/2 cups almond flour
- 1/3 cup unsalted butter, melted
- 3 tablespoons erythritol
- 1 teaspoon vanilla extract
- For the Filling:
- 24 ounces cream cheese, softened
- 1 cup erythritol
- 3 large eggs
- 1 cup sour cream
- 1 tablespoon lemon juice
- 1 teaspoon vanilla extract

For the Raspberry Swirl:
- 1/2 cup raspberries, fresh or frozen
- 2 tablespoons erythritol
- 1 teaspoon lemon juice

Instructions:

1. Preheat the oven to 325°F (163°C). Combine almond flour, melted butter, erythritol, and vanilla extract in a bowl. Mix until a crumbly dough forms. Press the mixture into the bottom of a 9-inch springform pan. Set aside.
2. In a small saucepan, combine raspberries, erythritol, and lemon juice. Cook over medium heat until the berries break down and the mixture thickens slightly, about 5-7 minutes. Strain through a fine mesh to remove seeds and set aside to cool.
3. Beat the cream cheese and erythritol together until smooth. Add eggs one at a time, fully incorporating each before adding the next. Mix in sour cream, lemon juice, and vanilla extract until the filling is smooth and well combined.
4. Pour the cheesecake filling over the prepared crust. Drop spoonfuls of the raspberry sauce over the filling. Use a toothpick or knife to swirl the sauce into the filling. Tap the pan on the counter a few times to remove any air bubbles.
5. Bake in the preheated oven for 50 minutes, or until the edges are set but the center still jiggles slightly. Turn off the oven, open the oven door slightly, and let the cheesecake cool in the oven for 1 hour.
6. Remove the cheesecake from the oven and let it cool to room temperature. Then refrigerate for at least 4 hours, or overnight.

Nutritional Information (Per Serving):

Calories: 350 | Protein: 8 g | Carbohydrates: 6 g
Fats: 32 g | Cholesterol: 120 mg | Sodium: 220 mg
Potassium: 90 mg

Keto Tiramisu

 Yield: 8 servings

Preparation Time: 30 minutes

Cooking Time: 4 hours

Ingredients:

For the Keto Sponge Cake:
- 1 cup almond flour
- 1/4 cup coconut flour
- 1/3 cup erythritol or other keto-friendly sweetener
- 1 teaspoon baking powder
- 4 large eggs, separated
- 1/4 cup unsalted butter, melted
- 1 teaspoon vanilla extract

For the Coffee Mixture:
- 1/2 cup strong brewed coffee, cooled
- 1 tablespoon coffee liqueur (optional, can use coffee-flavored syrup for a non-alcoholic version)

For the Mascarpone Cream:
- 1 1/2 cups mascarpone cheese
- 1 cup heavy cream
- 1/4 cup erythritol
- 1 teaspoon vanilla extract

Instructions:

1. Preheat your oven to 350°F (175°C). Line a rectangular baking dish or a large baking sheet with parchment paper. In a bowl, combine almond flour, coconut flour, erythritol, and baking powder. In a separate bowl, whisk egg yolks with melted butter and vanilla extract. Stir this into the dry ingredients. In another bowl, beat egg whites until stiff peaks form. Gently fold into the batter to keep it light and airy. Spread the batter evenly onto the prepared baking dish. Bake for 18-20 minutes or until golden and cooked through. Let cool completely.
2. Combine cooled coffee with coffee liqueur or syrup in a shallow dish.
3. In a mixing bowl, combine mascarpone cheese, heavy cream, erythritol, and vanilla extract. Beat until the mixture is smooth and creamy.
4. Assemble the Tiramisu: Slice the sponge cake into ladyfinger-sized strips. Briefly dip each piece into the coffee mixture and layer them in a serving dish. Spread half of the mascarpone cream over the first layer of soaked cake. Add another layer of soaked cake and top with the remaining mascarpone cream. Smooth the top and cover. Chill in the refrigerator for at least 4 hours, or overnight to set.

Nutritional Information (Per Serving):

Calories: 450 | Protein: 9 g | Carbohydrates: 8 g
Fats: 42 g | Cholesterol: 180 mg | Sodium: 120 mg
Potassium: 100 mg

Pumpkin Spice Latte Cupcakes

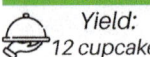 **Yield:** 12 cupcakes **Preparation Time:** 20 minutes **Cooking Time:** 20 minutes

Ingredients:

For the Cupcakes:
- 1 1/2 cups almond flour
- 1/4 cup coconut flour
- 1/2 cup erythritol (or another keto-friendly sweetener)
- 2 teaspoons baking powder
- 1 tablespoon pumpkin pie spice
- 1/2 teaspoon salt
- 3 large eggs
- 1 cup canned pumpkin puree

- 1/4 cup unsalted butter, melted
- 1/4 cup unsweetened almond milk
- 1 teaspoon vanilla extract
- 2 teaspoons instant coffee powder (dissolved in 1 tablespoon hot water)

For the Frosting:
- 8 ounces cream cheese, softened
- 1/4 cup unsalted butter, softened
- 1/3 cup erythritol (powdered)
- 1 teaspoon vanilla extract

Instructions:

1. Preheat the oven to 350°F (175°C). Line a 12-cup muffin tin with cupcake liners.
2. In a large bowl, whisk together almond flour, coconut flour, erythritol, baking powder, pumpkin pie spice, and salt. In another bowl, mix the eggs, pumpkin puree, melted butter, almond milk, vanilla extract, and dissolved coffee. Gradually add the wet ingredients to the dry ingredients, stirring until just combined. Avoid overmixing to keep the texture light.
3. Bake: Divide the batter evenly among the prepared cupcake liners, filling each about 3/4 full. Bake in the preheated oven for 18-20 minutes, or until a toothpick inserted into the center of a cupcake comes out clean.
4. Prepare the Frosting: While the cupcakes are baking, beat the cream cheese and butter together until smooth. Add the powdered erythritol and vanilla extract and continue to beat until creamy.
5. Cool and Frost: Allow the cupcakes to cool in the pan for about 5 minutes, then transfer to a wire rack to cool completely. Once cool, frost each cupcake with the cream cheese frosting.

Nutritional Information (Per Serving):

Calories: 280 | Protein: 7 g | Carbohydrates: 8 g
Fats: 25 g | Cholesterol: 85 mg | Sodium: 220 mg
Potassium: 150 mg

Keto Blondies

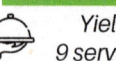 **Yield:** 9 servings 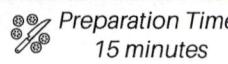 **Preparation Time:** 15 minutes  **Cooking Time:** 25 minutes

Ingredients:

- 1/2 cup unsalted butter, melted
- 1 cup almond flour
- 1/3 cup coconut flour
- 3/4 cup erythritol (or another keto-friendly sweetener)
- 2 large eggs
- 2 teaspoons vanilla extract
- 1/2 teaspoon baking powder
- 1/4 teaspoon salt
- 1/2 cup sugar-free chocolate chips

Instructions:

1. Preheat your oven to 350°F (175°C). Line an 8x8 inch baking dish with parchment paper or lightly grease it.
2. In a medium bowl, whisk together almond flour, coconut flour, baking powder, and salt. In a large bowl, mix the melted butter and erythritol until well combined. Beat in the eggs and vanilla extract until smooth. Gradually add the dry ingredients to the wet ingredients, stirring until well combined. Fold in the sugar-free chocolate chips.
3. Bake the Blondies: Pour the batter into the prepared baking dish, spreading it evenly. Bake in the preheated oven for 25 minutes or until the edges are golden and a toothpick inserted into the center comes out clean.
4. Cool and Serve: Let the blondies cool in the pan for about 10 minutes before lifting them out using the parchment paper (if used). Transfer to a wire rack to cool completely. Once cooled, cut into 9 squares.

Nutritional Information (Per Serving):

Calories: 220 | Protein: 5 g | Carbohydrates: 8 g
Fats: 20 g | Cholesterol: 55 mg | Sodium: 75 mg
Potassium: 100 mg

Coconut Chocolate Truffles

🍽 Yield: 20 truffles | ✳ Preparation Time: 15 minutes | ❄ Chilling Time: 1 hour

Ingredients:

For the Truffle Center:
- 1 cup unsweetened shredded coconut
- 1/2 cup coconut cream
- 1/4 cup erythritol (powdered)
- 1 teaspoon vanilla extract

For the Chocolate Coating:
- 1/2 cup sugar-free dark chocolate chips
- 1 tablespoon coconut oil

Optional for Garnish:
- Extra shredded coconut, toasted
- Cocoa powder

Instructions:

1. Prepare the Truffle Mixture: In a food processor, combine shredded coconut, coconut cream, powdered erythritol, and vanilla extract. Blend until the mixture is well combined and sticky. Using a spoon, scoop out small amounts of the mixture and roll into balls about 1 inch in diameter. Place on a parchment-lined baking sheet.
2. Chill the Truffles: Refrigerate the truffle centers for about 30 minutes to firm up.
3. In a microwave-safe bowl, combine the dark chocolate chips and coconut oil. Microwave in 30-second bursts, stirring between each burst, until the chocolate is completely melted and smooth.
4. Dip each chilled truffle center into the melted chocolate, ensuring it is fully coated. Use a fork to lift the truffle out of the chocolate, allowing excess chocolate to drip off. Return the coated truffles to the parchment paper. If using, sprinkle with toasted coconut or dust with cocoa powder while the chocolate is still melted.
5. Chill to Set: Refrigerate the coated truffles for another 30 minutes or until the chocolate coating is firm.

Nutritional Information (Per Serving):

Calories: 80 | Protein: 1 g | Carbohydrates: 3 g
Fats: 7 g | Cholesterol: 0 mg | Sodium: 5 mg
Potassium: 30 mg

Keto Key Lime Pie

🍽 Yield: 8 servings | ✳ Preparation Time: 20 minutes | Cooking Time: 15 minutes

Ingredients:

For the Crust:
- 1 1/2 cups almond flour
- 1/3 cup unsalted butter, melted
- 3 tablespoons erythritol
- 1 teaspoon vanilla extract

For the Filling:
- 1 cup heavy cream
- 8 ounces cream cheese, softened
- 1/2 cup erythritol (powdered for smoother texture)
- 1/2 cup key lime juice (freshly squeezed or bottled)
- Zest of 2 key limes
- 1 teaspoon vanilla extract

Optional for Garnish:
- Whipped cream (keto-friendly)

Instructions:

1. Preheat the oven to 350°F (175°C). Combine almond flour, melted butter, erythritol, and vanilla extract in a bowl. Mix until a dough forms. Press the mixture into the bottom and up the sides of a 9-inch pie pan to form the crust. Bake in the preheated oven for 10-12 minutes, or until golden. Remove and let cool.
2. In a large mixing bowl, beat the cream cheese until smooth. Add erythritol, lime zest, lime juice, and vanilla extract. Mix until well combined. In a separate bowl, whip the heavy cream until stiff peaks form. Gently fold the whipped cream into the lime mixture until fully incorporated.
3. Assemble the Pie: Pour the filling into the cooled crust and smooth the top with a spatula. Chill the pie in the refrigerator for at least 2 hours or until set.
4. Garnish and Serve: Just before serving, garnish with keto-friendly whipped cream.

Nutritional Information (Per Serving):

Calories: 410 | Protein: 7 g | Carbohydrates: 8 g
Fats: 40 g | Cholesterol: 80 mg | Sodium: 200 mg
Potassium: 90 mg

Salted Caramel Pudding

 **Yield:** 6 servings   **Preparation Time:** 10 minutes   **Cooking Time:** 15 minutes

Ingredients:

For the Salted Caramel:
- 1/2 cup erythritol
- 2 tablespoons water
- 1/2 cup heavy cream
- 2 tablespoons unsalted butter
- 1/2 teaspoon sea salt

For the Pudding:
- 2 cups heavy cream
- 3 large egg yolks
- 1 teaspoon vanilla extract
- Additional pinch of sea salt

For Garnish:
- Whipped cream (keto-friendly)
- A sprinkle of sea salt

Instructions:

1. In a medium saucepan over medium heat, combine erythritol and water. Stir until the erythritol dissolves, then cook without stirring until the mixture becomes a golden-brown caramel color, about 5-7 minutes. Carefully add the heavy cream (the mixture will bubble) and stir until smooth. Add the butter and salt, stirring until the butter is melted and the mixture is smooth. Remove from heat.
2. In a separate bowl, whisk the egg yolks and vanilla extract. Slowly pour about a third of the hot caramel into the egg yolks while whisking continuously to temper the eggs. Transfer the tempered egg mixture back into the saucepan with the remaining caramel. Cook over low heat, stirring constantly, until the mixture thickens enough to coat the back of a spoon, about 5 minutes.
3. Remove the pudding mixture from heat. If desired, strain through a fine-mesh sieve to remove any lumps and ensure a smooth texture.
4. Pour the pudding into serving dishes. Cover with plastic wrap, pressing it directly onto the surface of the pudding to prevent a skin from forming. Chill in the refrigerator for at least 2 hours.
5. Before serving, top each pudding with a dollop of whipped cream, a sprinkle of sea salt.

Nutritional Information (Per Serving):

Calories: 400 | Protein: 3 g | Carbohydrates: 4 g
Fats: 40 g | Cholesterol: 180 mg | Sodium: 220 mg
Potassium: 90 mg

Snickerdoodle Cream Cookies

 Yield: 12 servings   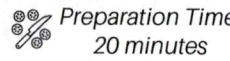 **Preparation Time:** 20 minutes   **Cooking Time:** 12 minutes

Ingredients:

For the Cookies:
- 2 cups almond flour
- 1/2 cup erythritol (granular)
- 1 teaspoon cream of tartar
- 1/2 teaspoon baking soda
- 1/4 teaspoon salt
- 1 teaspoon ground cinnamon
- 1/2 cup unsalted butter, softened
- 1 large egg
- 2 teaspoons vanilla extract

For the Cinnamon Sugar Coating:
- 2 tablespoons erythritol (granular)
- 1 teaspoon ground cinnamon

For the Cream Filling:
- 1/2 cup heavy cream
- 4 ounces cream cheese, softened
- 1/4 cup powdered erythritol
- 1 teaspoon vanilla extract

Instructions:

1. In a large bowl, whisk together almond flour, erythritol, cream of tartar, baking soda, salt, and cinnamon. In another bowl, cream the butter using an electric mixer until light and fluffy. Beat in the egg and vanilla extract. Gradually mix the dry ingredients into the wet ingredients until a dough forms.
2. Cover the dough with plastic wrap and refrigerate for at least 30 minutes.
3. Preheat your oven to 350°F (175°C). Line a baking sheet with parchment paper. Mix 2 tablespoons erythritol and 1 teaspoon cinnamon in a small bowl for the coating.
4. Remove the dough from the fridge. Roll into small balls, then roll each ball in the cinnamon sugar mixture. Place on the prepared baking sheet and flatten slightly. Bake for 10-12 minutes or until the edges are just turning brown. Remove from the oven and let cool on the pan for 5 minutes before transferring to a wire rack to cool completely.
5. While cookies cool, whip the heavy cream until it forms stiff peaks. In another bowl, beat the cream cheese with powdered erythritol and vanilla extract until smooth. Fold the whipped cream into the cream cheese mixture until combined.
6. Once cookies are cooled, spread or pipe the cream filling on the flat side of a cookie and sandwich with another cookie.

Nutritional Information (Per Serving):

Calories: 320 | Protein: 6 g | Carbohydrates: 7 g
Fats: 29 g | Cholesterol: 70 mg | Sodium: 150 mg
Potassium: 50 mg

Blackberry Cobbler

 Yield:
8 servings

Preparation Time:
15 minutes

Cooking Time:
25 minutes

Ingredients:

- For the Filling:
- 3 cups fresh blackberries
- 1/4 cup erythritol
- 1 teaspoon vanilla extract
- 1/2 teaspoon ground cinnamon
- For the Topping:
- 1 cup almond flour
- 1/4 cup coconut flour
- 1/4 cup erythritol
- 1/2 teaspoon baking powder
- 1/4 cup cold unsalted butter, cubed
- 1 large egg, beaten
- Optional: 1/4 cup chopped pecans or walnuts for extra crunch

Instructions:

1. Preheat your oven to 375°F (190°C). In a mixing bowl, combine blackberries, erythritol, vanilla extract, and cinnamon. Toss gently to coat the berries evenly. Pour the berry mixture into an 8x8-inch baking dish, spreading it out evenly.
2. In another bowl, mix almond flour, coconut flour, erythritol, and baking powder. Add the cubed butter to the dry ingredients. Use a pastry cutter or your fingers to blend the butter into the flour until the mixture resembles coarse crumbs. Stir in the beaten egg (and optional nuts) until the mixture is just combined and crumbly.
3. Sprinkle the topping evenly over the blackberry mixture in the baking dish. Place the dish in the preheated oven and bake for 25 minutes, or until the topping is golden brown and the blackberry filling is bubbling.
4. Remove the cobbler from the oven and let it cool slightly before serving.

Nutritional Information (Per Serving):

Calories: 210 | Protein: 5 g | Carbohydrates: 12 g
Fats: 18 g | Cholesterol: 40 mg | Sodium: 50 mg
Potassium: 135 mg

SAUCES AND DRESSINGS

Keto-friendly additions to enhance any meal.

Cilantro Lime Dressing

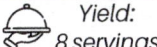 **Yield:**
8 servings

 **Preparation Time:**
10 minutes

 Total Time:
10 minutes

Ingredients:
- 1 cup fresh cilantro leaves, tightly packed
- 1/2 cup olive oil
- 1/4 cup lime juice (freshly squeezed)
- 2 tablespoons apple cider vinegar
- 1 clove garlic
- 1/2 teaspoon salt
- 1/4 teaspoon ground black pepper

Instructions:
1. Wash the cilantro leaves thoroughly and pat them dry. Squeeze fresh limes to make 1/4 cup of juice. Peel the garlic clove.
2. In a blender or food processor, combine cilantro, olive oil, lime juice, apple cider vinegar, garlic, salt, and black pepper. Blend on high speed until the mixture is smooth and emulsified.
3. Taste the dressing and adjust the seasoning if necessary. If it's too thick, add a little water or more lime juice to thin it out to your desired consistency.
4. Use immediately or store in an airtight container in the refrigerator for up to 1 week.

Keto Barbecue Sauce

Yield:
16 servings

 Preparation Time:
5 minutes

Cooking Time:
20 minutes

(2 tablespoons per serving)

Ingredients:
- 1 cup tomato sauce (unsweetened)
- 1/4 cup apple cider vinegar
- 1/4 cup erythritol (granular)
- 2 tablespoons Worcestershire sauce (sugar-free)
- 1 tablespoon smoked paprika
- 1 tablespoon garlic powder
- 1 tablespoon onion powder
- 1/2 teaspoon ground black pepper
- 1/2 teaspoon sea salt
- Optional: 1 teaspoon liquid smoke for a smokier flavor

Instructions:
1. In a medium saucepan, combine tomato sauce, apple cider vinegar, erythritol, Worcestershire sauce, smoked paprika, garlic powder, onion powder, black pepper, and sea salt. If using, add the cayenne pepper and liquid smoke.
2. Place the saucepan over medium heat and bring the mixture to a simmer. Stir frequently to ensure the erythritol dissolves completely and the flavors meld together.
3. Reduce the heat to low and let the sauce simmer gently for about 15-20 minutes, or until it has thickened to your desired consistency. Stir occasionally to prevent sticking.
4. Taste the barbecue sauce and adjust the seasoning if necessary, adding more salt, pepper.
5. Remove the sauce from heat and allow it to cool. Transfer to an airtight container and refrigerate.

Nutritional Information (Per Serving):
Calories: 140 | Protein: 0 g | Carbohydrates: 1 g
Fats: 15 g | Cholesterol: 0 mg | Sodium: 150 mg
Potassium: 20 mg

Nutritional Information (Per Serving):
Calories: 15 | Protein: 0.5 g | Carbohydrates: 3 g
Fats: 0 g | Cholesterol: 0 mg | Sodium: 150 mg
Potassium: 90 mg

Lemon Tahini Dressing

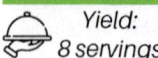 **Yield:** 8 servings   **Preparation Time:** 10 minutes **Total Time:** 10 minutes

Ingredients:
- 1/2 cup tahini (sesame seed paste)
- 1/4 cup olive oil
- Juice of 2 lemons (about 1/4 cup)
- 2 cloves garlic, minced
- 1/2 teaspoon salt, or to taste
- 1/4 teaspoon black pepper
- 1/4 cup warm water (adjust for desired consistency)
- Optional: 1 tablespoon chopped fresh parsley or cilantro for garnish

Instructions:
1. In a medium bowl, whisk together tahini, olive oil, and lemon juice until well blended. Add the minced garlic, salt, and black pepper. Continue whisking until all ingredients are well incorporated.
2. Gradually add warm water while whisking, a tablespoon at a time, until the dressing reaches your desired consistency. It should be creamy but pourable.
3. Taste the dressing and adjust the seasoning as needed, adding more salt or lemon juice according to your preference.
4. Stir in optional chopped parsley or cilantro just before serving for added flavor and a pop of color.
5. Use immediately, or store in an airtight container in the refrigerator for up to 5 days. Stir well before using if the dressing thickens upon chilling.

Nutritional Information (Per Serving):
Calories: 140 | Protein: 3 g | Carbohydrates: 3 g
Fats: 13 g | Cholesterol: 0 mg | Sodium: 150 mg
Potassium: 50 mg

Keto Gravy

 Yield: 8 servings 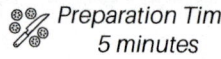 **Preparation Time:** 5 minutes   **Cooking Time:** 15 minutes

Ingredients:
- 1/4 cup unsalted butter
- 1/4 cup heavy cream
- 1 cup beef or chicken broth
- 2 teaspoons xanthan gum (for thickening)
- 1/2 teaspoon garlic powder
- 1/2 teaspoon onion powder
- Salt and pepper to taste
- Optional: Fresh herbs (such as thyme or rosemary) for added flavor

Instructions:
1. In a saucepan over medium heat, melt the butter. Slowly whisk in the broth to the melted butter, ensuring it blends well. Add garlic powder, onion powder, and any optional fresh herbs. Stir to combine.
2. Sprinkle xanthan gum over the mixture while continuously whisking to prevent clumping. Keep whisking until the gravy begins to thicken, about 5-7 minutes.
3. Reduce heat to low and let the gravy simmer for a few more minutes to reach your desired consistency. If the gravy is too thick, add a little more broth to thin it out.
4. Taste and adjust the seasoning with salt and pepper.
5. Serve the gravy hot over your favorite keto dishes.

Nutritional Information (Per Serving):
Calories: 80 | Protein: 0.5 g | Carbohydrates: 0.5 g
Fats: 8 g | Cholesterol: 20 mg | Sodium: 150 mg
Potassium: 10 mg

Tomato Basil Marinara Sauce

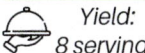 Yield:
8 servings

 Preparation Time:
10 minutes

 Cooking Time:
30 minutes

Ingredients:

- 1/4 cup olive oil
- 3 cloves garlic, minced
- 1 can (28 ounces) crushed tomatoes (no added sugar)
- 1/4 cup fresh basil leaves, chopped
- 1 teaspoon dried oregano
- Salt and pepper to taste

Instructions:

1. Heat the olive oil in a large skillet or saucepan over medium heat. Add the minced garlic. Sauté until the onion is translucent and garlic is fragrant, about 3-5 minutes.
2. Stir in the crushed tomatoes. Reduce heat slightly and let the tomatoes simmer for about 20 minutes, stirring occasionally.
3. Add the chopped basil, dried oregano, salt, and pepper. If using, add red pepper flakes and sweetener. Stir well to combine all the ingredients.
4. Continue to simmer the sauce for an additional 10 minutes. This will allow the flavors to meld together and the sauce to thicken slightly.
5. Taste the sauce and adjust seasoning as needed. More salt may be needed depending on your preference and the acidity of the tomatoes.
6. Use the sauce immediately over your favorite keto dishes or allow it to cool and store in an airtight container in the refrigerator for up to a week.

Buffalo Sauce

 Yield:
1 cup

Preparation Time:
5 minutes

 Cooking Time:
10 minutes

Ingredients:

- 1/2 cup unsalted butter
- 1/3 cup hot sauce (like Frank's Red-Hot Sauce, which is naturally low in carbs)
- 1 tablespoon apple cider vinegar
- 1/2 teaspoon Worcestershire sauce (check for a sugar-free version)
- 1/4 teaspoon garlic powder
- 1/4 teaspoon cayenne pepper (adjust based on heat preference)
- Salt to taste

Instructions:

1. In a small saucepan, melt the butter over medium heat.
2. Once the butter is melted, reduce the heat to low and add the hot sauce, apple cider vinegar, Worcestershire sauce, garlic powder, and cayenne pepper. Stir to combine all the ingredients thoroughly.
3. Allow the mixture to simmer for 5-10 minutes, stirring occasionally to ensure the flavors meld together. The sauce should thicken slightly.
4. Taste the sauce and adjust the seasoning with additional cayenne pepper or salt, if needed.
5. Remove from heat and let the sauce cool to room temperature. It can be used immediately or stored in an airtight container in the refrigerator for up to two weeks.

Nutritional Information (Per Serving):

Calories: 90 | Protein: 2 g | Carbohydrates: 6 g
Fats: 7 g | Cholesterol: 0 mg | Sodium: 300 mg
Potassium: 350 mg

Nutritional Information (Per Serving):

Calories: 50 | Protein: 0 g | Carbohydrates: 0.5 g
Fats: 5.5 g | Cholesterol: 15 mg | Sodium: 100 mg
Potassium: 10 mg

Pesto Sauce

 Yield:
8 servings

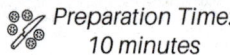 **Preparation Time:**
10 minutes

Ingredients:

- 2 cups fresh basil leaves, packed
- 1/2 cup grated Parmesan cheese
- 1/2 cup extra virgin olive oil
- 1/3 cup pine nuts (could substitute walnuts or almonds for different flavors)
- 2 garlic cloves, peeled
- Salt and pepper to taste
- Optional: 1 tablespoon lemon juice for added brightness

Instructions:

1. Wash the basil leaves thoroughly and pat them dry. In a food processor, combine the basil leaves, Parmesan cheese, pine nuts, and garlic cloves. Pulse a few times to chop and blend the ingredients.
2. With the processor running, slowly pour in the olive oil in a steady stream. This helps to emulsify the oil and incorporate it fully into the basil mixture.
3. Once the mixture is smooth, season with salt and pepper. Add lemon juice if using. Pulse a few more times to mix thoroughly.
4. If the pesto is too thick, add more olive oil in small amounts until you reach your desired consistency.
5. Taste the pesto and adjust the seasoning as needed, adding more salt, pepper, or lemon juice to suit your taste.

Nutritional Information (Per Serving):

Calories: 200 | Protein: 3 g | Carbohydrates: 2 g
Fats: 20 g | Cholesterol: 4 mg | Sodium: 100 mg
Potassium: 50 mg

Hollandaise Sauce

 Yield:
4 servings

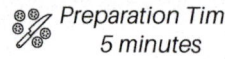 **Preparation Time:**
5 minutes

 Cooking Time:
5 minutes

Ingredients:

- 4 large egg yolks
- 1 tablespoon lemon juice (freshly squeezed)
- 1/2 cup unsalted butter (1 stick), melted and hot
- 1/2 teaspoon Dijon mustard (optional, for added flavor)
- Pinch of cayenne pepper (optional, for a slight kick)
- Salt and black pepper to taste

Instructions:

1. Fill a saucepan with about 1-2 inches of water and bring it to a simmer over medium heat. Place a heatproof bowl (preferably stainless steel) over the simmering water, making sure the bottom of the bowl does not touch the water.
2. In the heatproof bowl, add the 4 large egg yolks and whisk them continuously for about 1-2 minutes until they become slightly thickened.
3. Add the tablespoon of freshly squeezed lemon juice, a pinch of salt, and black pepper (to taste). If using Dijon mustard or cayenne pepper, whisk these in at this stage. Continue whisking until the mixture is smooth and well-combined.
4. Slowly drizzle the hot, melted butter into the egg yolk mixture while constantly whisking. Start with a very slow stream, and as the sauce begins to thicken, you can increase the butter flow. This process should take about 3 minutes.
5. Once all the butter is incorporated, the Hollandaise sauce should be thick and smooth. If the sauce becomes too thick, you can add a small amount of warm water (1 teaspoon at a time) to achieve the desired consistency.
6. Taste the sauce and adjust with additional salt, pepper, or lemon juice if needed.

Nutritional Information (Per Serving):

Calories: 220 kcal | Protein: 2g | Carbohydrates: 1g
Fat: 24g | Cholesterol: 230mg | Sodium: 120mg
Potassium: 25mg

CHAPTER 9
SHOPPING LIST AND INDEX

Grocery List

Protein Sources:
» Eggs
» Salmon (fresh or smoked)
» Shrimp
» Chicken breasts and thighs
» Ground beef
» Bacon
» Turkey
» Pork (sausage, ground, chops)
» Lamb chops
» Cod and Tilapia
» Duck breast

Dairy and Dairy Alternatives:
» Heavy cream
» Cream cheese
» Mozzarella cheese (shredded and slices)
» Cheddar cheese
» Parmesan cheese
» Butter (grass-fed)
» Sour cream
» Greek yogurt (unsweetened, full-fat)
» Almond milk (unsweetened)

Vegetables:
» Avocados
» Broccoli
» Cauliflower
» Zucchini
» Mixed salad greens
» Spinach
» Bell peppers
» Asparagus
» Mushrooms
» Eggplant
» Green beans
» Cabbage
» Lettuce
» Tomatoes (fresh and cherry)
» Garlic
» Onions
» Cucumber

Fruits (low-carb):
» Blueberries
» Raspberries
» Lemons
» Limes

Pantry and Baking:
» Almond flour
» Coconut flour
» Erythritol or other keto-friendly sweeteners
» Baking powder
» Vanilla extract
» Cocoa powder
» Coconut oil
» Olive oil
» Vinegars (balsamic, red wine)
» Canned pumpkin
» Coconut cream
» Canned tuna
» Almond butter
» Various herbs and spices (paprika, thyme, rosemary, dill, etc.)

Nuts and Seeds:
» Almonds
» Macadamia nuts
» Pecans
» Chia seeds

Sauces and Condiments:
» Soy sauce or coconut aminos
» Mustard
» Sugar-free ketchup
» Mayonnaise
» Hot sauce
» Pesto
» Sugar-free marinara sauce

Additional Items:
» Keto-friendly wraps (like cauliflower)
» Low-carb bread (like cloud bread)
» Fish sauce
» Wine (for cooking)

Index

YOUR FREE GIFT!

Scan the QR code to download

Your free E-Book gift.

Dive into delightful recipes that are sure to inspire your culinary journey!

Printed in Great Britain
by Amazon